HYPNO-HOG'S
MOONSHINE MONSTER
JAMBOREE

Andrew Goldfarb resides in San Francisco, where he draws the long-running underground comic strip "Ogner Stump's One Thousand Sorrows," which tells of the trials and tribulations of everyman Ogner Stump and his blue mutant sidekick, Slub Glub. He also travels the country performing as a one-man-surrealistic-rock-and-roll band under the name The Slow Poisoner. His previous books include *The Ballad of a Slow Poisoner* and *Slub Glub in the Weird World of the Weeping Willows*. He will plunge to his death over Niagara Falls in 2068.

HYPNO-HOG'S MOONSHINE MONSTER JAMBOREE

ANDREW GOLDFARB

ERASERHEAD PRESS
PORTLAND, OREGON

ERASERHEAD PRESS
205 NE BRYANT STREET
PORTLAND, OR 97211

WWW.ERASERHEADPRESS.COM

ISBN: 1-936383-98-5

Dedicated to Coco
(? – 2011)

The guinea pig who was worth his weight in gold.

CHAPTER 1

FARMER SLOGG AND THE SKULL-HEADED FROGS

Farmer Slogg woke up in an outhouse. His head rested on the seat plank, only inches from the circular hole that led to the dark swamp below. Since the outhouse was not as wide as Farmer Slogg was long, he had slept with his legs splayed up against the door, his toes poking through the crescent moon that was carved in the side. The toxic odor of human refuse, expected in an outhouse but nevertheless unpleasant to smell first thing in the morning, made its way to Farmer Slogg's hairy nostrils, and, in combination with the slivers of sunlight that poked through the sides of the wooden shack, thrust Herconium Siliam Slogg back to consciousness for another day of life on God's green Earth.

He brushed a cluster of dung beetles from his brow and unstuck his hands from the newspapers that lined the dirt floor. Digging his fingernails into the narrow wooden walls, he hauled himself to his feet with a groan. He scratched his head, inserted a wad of chewing tobacco into his gums, and listened to his stomach rumble. "Guess I'll eat myself an ear," he muttered, and he flung open the outhouse door.

Farmer Slogg's outhouse was perched at the top of a hill that occupied the far end of Farmer Slogg's Hog Farm. His herd of pigs numbered roughly thirteen, depending on how many had perished from fevers and how many had produced more piglets during the long country night. Though the pigpen was only a yard or two down the hill, the path was treacherous;

the surface of Slogg's hilltop was writhing with grubs and bloodworms; a seething, slithering mass of parasites that covered the entire slope.

"Dang these tiny serpents," Slogg muttered, gangling hurriedly out of the outhouse and down towards the pigpen. Slogg had only one good leg, which was his left one. On the right, he had been born with a hoof, which proved to be somewhat of a blessing, as the worms were unable to do any damage to the hoof. However, the toes of the left foot, which knew not the safety and protection of a shoe, were quickly feasted upon by the slimy assailants. Slogg knew from experience that he had less then a minute to make it to the safety of the pigpen before these minuscule fiends ate their way past the layers of caked dirt and debris on his heel and chewed their way into his skin. He went as fast as he could.

After a few minutes of sliding and stumbling, Slogg reached the wooden fence that surrounded his pigs, and hopped onto it, landing on his crotch. Slogg inspected his foot; a few enterprising grubs had burrowed beneath his toenails and were making their way under the cover of skin towards his ankle. "Oh no ya don't," he spat, rubbing the flesh of his ankle furiously, listening for the sound of the worms being squeezed to death beneath his skin. He continued rubbing until there was no more wriggling, satisfied that he had exterminated the intruders.

All thirteen pigs were asleep, with their backs in the muddy dirt and their little pink hooves in the air, dreaming the unknown dreams of pigs. Farmer Slogg climbed down and walked among them, furrowing his brow as he inspected their ears. If any ears were large enough, or if Slogg felt hungry enough, he would tear one off with Daisy, the serrated knife that dangled from the rope around his trousers. The ear would then be dipped into a pot of Slogg's World-Famous Frying Batter that stood in one corner of the pen.

This batter had made his family wealthy once. The fire

beneath the iron bucket that held the bubbling grease was always burning, and had been since Great-Grandfather Euphonious Slogg had first started frying pigs' ears back in 1906. In fact, the whole valley was named Slogg's Holler after Euphonious Slogg, such was the fame that Euphonious' recipe for fried pigs' ears had garnered back in the day. The crunchy delicacies were sold in an orange tin graced with images of nude faeries dancing. Beneath the frying cauldron, flames licked upwards from a fissure in the earth, and on the one occasion that Farmer Slogg had tried to extinguish it in a drunken fit (by pouring a bucket of tobacco spit over the purple flames) the fire had exploded into a great ball that singed every hair on Farmer Slogg's back, leaving him with a burn scar that closely resembled the intestinal tract of a skunk. But the fire had not gone out.

Behind the pigpen stood the remains of the Slogg Homestead – a reminder of the faded Slogg Fortune that this fry batter (and a thousand boiled hogs' ears) had once built. When Farmer Slogg was a boy, the Slogg Clan made their home in this columned house, but after Pa Slogg got stuck in a hay baler and subsequently eaten by ghosts, and Ma Slogg ran off with a scarecrow, the care and upkeep of the structure fell into the hands of young Herconium and his twelve brothers and sisters. These siblings had now departed from this planet. Over the years, each of them had the misfortune to stumble into the foul waters of Slogg's Creek, which skirted the perimeter of the farm. Speculation was that Slogg's Creek was plagued with devil-fish who dined on the Slogg siblings, sucking their souls down into the creekbed, as none of them were ever heard from again.

The lone exception was Farmer Slogg, who would have gladly joined his brothers and sisters in sinking drunkenly to his doom, but his gimp leg could never carry him quite that far. Slogg's entire right leg was nearly identical to that of a goat, down to the cloven hoof. When Herconium was born,

ANDREW GOLDFARB

Papa Euphonious Slogg accused Ma of cheating, an accusation
that created a rift in their marriage. In any event, when Farmer
Slogg heard the siren song of Slogg's Creek, calling him to his
watery grave, he could only get so far as the manure pile, where
he inevitably stumbled and collapsed until morning.

With his family gone, the orphaned Farmer Slogg made an
attempt at maintaining the ancestral home but domesticity was
not his strong suit. Soon, a cadre of militant opossums had
laid claim to the house, and proved well-organized in rebuffing
Farmer Slogg's half-hearted attempts to reclaim his property.
Eventually, he gave up and moved into the outhouse, which
was not so different from sleeping in the manure pile.

Now, Farmer Slogg surveyed the snoring litter of pigs at his
feet, and judged none of their ears to be of a sizeable enough
girth to be worth dining on. But the heavens above were about
to provide for Farmer Slogg. The skies had sprouted a great big
cloud, and this floating shroud bristled with electric portent.
With a thunderous crack and a bolt of lightning, a weird green
rain started coming down.

Farmer Slogg thought that it was a hailstorm at first, but the
falling projectiles hit the ground with an unnerving crunching
sound. Lurching downward and peering closer, it was evident
that the sky was raining frogs on Slogg's Farm. This was not an
entirely unknown phenomenon in Slogg's Holler, but picking
one of the frogs up by its leg, Farmer Slogg inspected it and
found that the frog had a normal enough body but that its head
appeared to be more human than amphibian, though miniature,
and was devoid of skin. It was a fat, scaly frog topped with the
tiny grinning skull of a miniscule human being.

Farmer Slogg pondered the death's-head frog from the sky.
"So now the skies be rainin' down bone-headed toads, eh?" he
mused. He stared at the strange slimy thing in his hand. His
first impulse was to drop it back to the ground and think no
more of the matter. However, looking at its plump green legs,
a second idea came to him. He hobbled over to the cauldron

of cooking oil and dropped the strange critter in.

He watched it boil in the bubbling vat as its small, scaly legs turned a crispy brown. After a minute, Farmer Slogg retrieved the carcass from the vat; the batter had coated its skull-head with a golden layer of grease. He took a bite of its foot.

After the first swallow, his field of vision went entirely black. In his mind's eye, he pictured a cascade of snakes dripping down from the stars. They formed a spiral, circling down the drain of his brain. Slogg chewed some more. Then he popped the rest of one of the frog's legs into his mouth. His vision cleared; a metallic taste remained on his tongue. Farmer Slog was about to shrug his shoulders in a nonchalant fashion when an odd itch erupted on the side of his neck. For a moment it felt like the Devil's claw was raking across his collar.

Then, with a sickly popping sound, a second head erupted from Farmer Slogg's shoulder. It resembled Farmer Slogg, but was even homelier. Slogg's second head opened its mouth and, with a snaggly yellow tooth, bit the other leg off the fried, skull-headed toad. "Not bad," it said.

"Nope," replied Farmer Slogg's head number one, and the newly two-headed Farmer Slogg headed back towards the outhouse.

CHAPTER 2
WHITE LIGHTNIN', QUITE FRIGHTENIN'

The drizzle of death-headed toads continued through the overcast afternoon in Slogg's Holler. About a mile away from Slogg's farm (as the mole burrows) stood the hovel of one Horlope Charlip. Horlope was a vital member of the community, as he owned the still that fermented the rotgut elixir upon which the good folks of Slogg's Holler imbibed and thrived. Horlope's hooch, distilled in a wild apparatus of animal intestines, medical machinery, and a claw-footed lead bathtub, put a fire in the belly that illuminated most of the burg.

"Yeegawd!" Horlope shrieked, exposing his six teeth. Horlope had just sliced off his middle finger with a rusty Bowie knife. His newly freed finger rolled off the table and onto the dirt floor, where it was quickly eaten by Horlope's hound.

"Good 'un, Horlope! Now it's my turn." Phendle Trunket was sitting next to Horlope. Phendle was narrow-headed, as his mother had taken a steam iron to his skull when he was a baby in an effort to make him more handsome. It had worked; though ugly as sin now, as a baby he had been as ugly as Beelzebub himself. He reached out his hand for the knife.

Horlope laughed. "Shore," he said, handing over the bloody weapon. "But you ain't gonna top that." Phendle gripped the knife in his fist and put his other hand flat down on the kitchen table, where the two men and their cousin Kerth were sitting. With a determined grimace, Phendle brought the blade down six times towards his four fingers and gnarled burl of a thumb, and spiny splinters of wood flew up from the table below. Though he'd been aiming the knife to stab at his own digits, his coordination was greatly impaired at present, and no wounds were inflicted.

"Dang it all to hell," Phendle moaned.

"Hee hee hee, you couldn't hit a barn side with a Burmese bride," Horlope cackled, sucking on his bleeding hand.

The third man, Cousin Kerth, looked at Horlope and Phendle with disgust. "That ain't the way you play Mumbledy-Peg," he slurred.

Phendle held a clay jug over his head and felt the last drop of liquor drip onto his eyeball with a sizzle. "We gotta git more hooch," he grimaced.

The three men made their way outdoors to the still. This apparatus, of which Horlope was extremely proud, spanned the length of the entire briar patch behind his shack. A large, leaden bathtub with clawed feet was connected by a spiraling copper tube to an oblong metal canister that had once served as Horlope's grandmother's iron lung. He had appropriated the iron lung for the purposes of his industrious brewing while Grandma was still alive, but she had managed to survive without it. She could often be heard at midnight moaning in the thickets, her sorrowful sounds intermingling with bleats from the poor sheep that she used to replace her iron lung. This sheep she had partially disemboweled and then attached to her chest cavity with rose-weeds. Nature, in its wily way, had allowed their flesh to intermingle and they now shared the sheep's lungs for their every unpleasant breath, an arrangement that was satisfactory to neither party but to which no improvement or alteration was ever made.

Beneath this iron lung was a collection of raccoon pelts and snakewood flowers, which were ignited by a rusty flint from Horlope's pocket, causing the iron lung to glow with a reddish hue. The heat spread through the copper coil to the lead bathtub, the contents of which included rotten apples and roadkill, along with cooking oil and formaldehyde purloined from the Slogg's Holler Funeral Home, then mixed with any other fermentable ingredients on hand that could contribute to the blind drunk that the mountain dew of Horlope Charlip promised its imbiber.

This concoction then passed through the iron lung, its radioactive casing of X-ray film and luminous watch hands assisting the alchemical processes of the recipe. The resultant glowing extract made its way though the winding nuances of a goat bladder and adjoining large intestine, eventually dangling over the branch of a poplar tree, beneath which a hollowed bull skull (which Horlope claimed to have inherited from a matador on his mother's side) served as a funnel and spigot. Phendle was placing his jug to the horn to replenish his thirst, when Cousin Kerth looked to the sky and said, "Hold up a minute, it's rainin' toads."

Horlope and Phendle both squinted upward. With a choral "ker-plunk" a pair of frogs fell from the sky, landing on each of their noses. "Ha! You both got toad-faced," Cousin Kerth chortled. Then, squinting, he remarked solemnly, "And they got bone-man faces."

He plucked one of the strange critters from Phendle's nose and held it up in front of them. "A demon rained down from Hell," Phendle gasped, turning away in horror.

"Naw," said Horlope, "Hell's down there, not up there." He pointed his fingers in opposite directions. All three of them stood still as the strange cascade of frogs with tiny human skulls continued to fall around their feet. "Let's have that drink," Horlope finally said.

The three men turned back towards the still, but were dismayed to find that the claw-footed bathtub was now overflowing with the skull-headed frogs. "Them critters is in yer still," Phendle astutely observed.

"Screw it," Horlope muttered. He lit the pile of raccoon

pelts beneath the iron lung. As the bathwater started to boil, the toads started to dissolve in the tub, an audible cry emerging from their corpse-mouths that resembled the shrieking of a skinned cat. A faint mist rose from the tub as its contents made their way through the distilling process, through the copper coil to the iron lung, which glowed red as the luminous watch hands that lined its side rotated wildly. Finally, the goat bladder filled with a thick fluid that it discharged into the bull skull. Fluorescent green goop spewed out of its eyes, which Horlope collected into his clay jug. He took a sip.

Phendle and Cousin Kerth looked towards him expectantly. His eyes glazed over momentarily, and then he slowly licked his lips. Seeing that he had not expired on the spot, the other two quickly grabbed the jug and helped themselves to it as well.

"Tastes okay," Phendle said. A faint popping noise followed.

"What wuz that?" Cousin Kerth asked nervously.

"I think that wuz you," Phendle replied, and then he fell to the ground laughing.

"What's so funny?" Cousin Kerth demanded.

"Look at yer armpit," Phendle choked out, engulfed in hysterics. Cousin Kerth lifted his arm and was surprised to see a large, pulsating lump had suddenly grown where there ought to have been only a few strands of hair. An eye socket seemed to be embedded in the fleshy mass as well, though its lids were shut.

Cousin Kerth was defensive, "Well, look what's callin' the kettle black," he retorted. As Phendle attempted to pick himself off the floor, he discovered that a third arm was growing out of his belly, which made it much easier to get up. Erect again, he used this third arm to pick up the clay jug.

"Must be 'cause of them sky-frogs in the hooch," he said.

"Gimme that jug!" said Horlope, grabbing it from Phendle. Horlope's head had swelled massively, and purple boils were pulsating on his nose and chin. He put his mouth to the jug.

"You sure you wanna keep drinkin' it?" Cousin Kerth

asked, scratching his armpit, which now blinked back at him.

"Screw it," Horlope said again, taking a swig. One of the purple boils on his nose blossomed open, revealing a set of teeth inside. Spittle dripped from them, causing Phendle to fall to the ground laughing again. The jug was passed around a few more times; their minds swam in a euphoric sludge as their physical beings continued to grow and mutate with a profusion of popping sounds.

A half hour later, the jug was empty, and the intoxicated trio were virtually unrecognizable.

"You look like a turnip!" Horlope squealed, pointing to Cousin Kerth, who was indeed red and tumescent on top, though his lower limbs were glowing green and unduly numerous. His armpit had sprouted a small, sullen head, which mumbled in a foreign tongue. Phendle, still on the ground, was in a drunken stupor of religious zeal and had taken to praying to Cousin Kerth's armpit head, clasping his six hands together solemnly. He resembled a hunched, beatific beetle.

"I'm gettin' hungry," complained Cousin Kerth. The skull-frog moonshine had given him an appetite, the likes of which he had never known before. "Got any grub?" he asked Horlope.

"Nope," Horlope replied out of both mouths. Below his head of purple lumps and extra mouth, his chest had expanded gelatinously, the bloat of his stomach dripping down to the floor and obscuring his legs so that he resembled a child's toy that would bounce upright after being knocked down. "I'm hungry too," he said with a sinister air, and he rolled towards Phendle, who was still lost in mystical reverence. Horlope rotated forward and took a bite from Phendle's glowing green buttock.

"Dang it Horlope, don't you bite my ass!" Phendle yelled, though he felt no pain from missing the chunk of flesh that Horlope had swallowed. In swift retaliation, Phendle buried his head in Horlope's swollen belly and started chewing his way in. Cousin Kerth lifted his arm and joined the feast, as the growth in his armpit now sported teeth as well as eyes. His new mouth munched on Phendle's six hands while his old mouth engulfed Horlope's nose.

This hideous orgy of cannibal frenzy reached a fever pitch as Phendle disappeared entirely into Horlope's humongous torso, a torso that was in turn digested by Cousin Kerth's two famished mouths. The loss of his body in no way impeded the progress of Horlope's head, whose gnashing teeth managed to not only digest cousin Kerth entirely, but in a fantastic feat of eating, inverted its mouth and swallowed its own self. In the end, nothing remained of the three men but a puddle of drool and blood by the empty jug.

CHAPTER 3

BLEEDING MOON AND BACON BOUNTY

As night fell, skull-headed frogs continued to trickle down from pregnant clouds and land gently in the mud of Farmer Slogg's pigpen. These strange toads drowned in the trough of slop, and the pigs lapped them up, swallowing the slimy legs and skeletal heads along with the corncobs and peach peels they were accustomed to.

Shortly after digesting the skull-frog slop, the pigs underwent unusual changes in their minds and in their flesh. Firstly, their simple brains began to hallucinate. Of the thirteen pigs, the oldest and largest among them was the first to see that the moon had turned red and was starting to bleed. Soon the other dozen were gathered alongside him, their snouts pointed attentively upwards, entranced by the lunar pageant that unfolded as the amphibian-enhanced feed made its way from their hammy jaws to their bacon brains. The moon changed its hue from a mustard yellow to the pinkish shade of a beet, and sprouted holes like Swiss cheese that sprung torrents of red fluid, which fell to Earth, bathing the hogs in an unearthly cherry glow. Then their physical transformation began. They quivered and then swelled, rapidly expanding to nearly twice their size, jostling each other as the pigpen became suddenly crowded with plumped pork.

Some of the younger piglets squealed with anxiety at this development, but calm soon descended on the swine. The moon had gone back to being yellow and non-porous.

The eldest among them, the big boar, was now five-hundred pounds and six feet long after his growth spurt. As the other newly-enlarged pigs sank into the mud to sleep, he stared out across the horizon until the first rays of the sun poked out from behind the hill at the top of Slogg's farm. Then he went back to the trough for a second helping of the skull-frog slop.

When the next morning dawned, Euphonious Slogg awoke with a crick in both necks. His first head looked at the second and they nodded to each other. "Think I'll eat me an ear," they uttered in unison. Once unstuck from the outhouse floor, the new and improved Farmer Slogg ran madly over the landscape of evil worms to get down to his pigpen to see if there was something there he could eat; and this morning, unlike the last, there were pig ears a-plenty, supersized and succulent, flapping pinkly in the breeze, waving like ruddy flags.

"Sweet Lord in Heaven!" Farmer Slogg exclaimed from one of his mouths, and he fell down upon his knees in the mud. His pigpen was bursting at the seams with the swollen sows that had feasted on the strange amphibian rain of the night before, and aside from their greater girth, their heads had sprouted extra ears as well – most had six or seven (plus an additional snout or two). Slogg stared in bewilderment, then squeezed his way among the pigs to inspect each of them, marveling at this turn of events. He wondered if this was indeed a gift from God, or perhaps a moonshine delusion. Feeling the soft fleshy flap of a piglet's fourth ear between his fingers, he decided that it was the former, and turning both his heads to the heavens, Farmer Slogg offered a statement of gratitude to his mystical benefactor. "Dear Maker of All Above, I want to dearly thank thee for seeing fit to bestow on my humble litter a heap of extra helping with which to fill my belly and my boilin' pot." Then he reached for Daisy, his knife, and sliced off the hog's ears, all four of them. The pig oinked.

One by one, Herconium Slogg took Daisy around to each pig; they all gave an annoyed oink as the rusty knife sawed through their pink triangular ears, but they seemed to feel no pain and were only mildly inconvenienced. Making his way through the crammed pen, hacking away, Farmer Slogg collected thirty-seven ears from the first twelve pigs, which he stuffed into the pockets of his overalls. But when he came to the biggest boar, he stopped.

The elder hog, which had spent the night slurping up the remaining skull-head toads that had fallen from the sky, had swollen to the great girth of a thousand pounds, and he now took up the entire rear third of the pigpen. He was a pink mountain plopped down in the mud, and his demeanor was different from that of the other pigs in the pen, who were either sleeping or had their snouts deep in slop. The big boar was awake but unmoving, and eating as well, but on vegetables and fruits that were being brought to him by a succession of rabbits, skunks and raccoons, all of whom were lined up in an orderly fashion as if paying tribute to the great pig. This trail of creatures wound all the way down from the neighboring hills. Each animal had with it some sort of offering; the rabbits carried carrots in their paws, and the raccoons bore berries on their back, which they dropped at the base of the giant hog. Farmer Slogg gaped in amazement and confusion.

Then, regaining his senses, Euphonious eyed the huge hog's ears. Although they numbered only two, they were certainly the largest pigs' ears that Farmer Slogg had ever seen. He raised Daisy, still dripping with the blood of the other twelve hogs' thirty-seven amputated ears, and approached the great pigs' head…but was suddenly frozen in place. The big pig was watching Farmer Slogg, and his great bulbous pig eyes were dark and deep. A strange tickling sensation ruffled the back of Slogg's brain. Staring into the giant pig's eyes, Euphonious decided that he had enough ears for now, and would leave this one for tomorrow.

With that, he turned away and moved towards the pot of boiling batter to drop the pigs' ears in. Plenty of skull-headed frogs had fallen into the cauldron overnight as well; Farmer Slogg's World-Famous Frying Batter was bursting to the brim with more ingredients than it had seen in many moons. Filled with a rare satisfaction, Euphonious Slogg headed back up towards the outhouse while the ears and toads turned golden brown and crispy.

CHAPTER 4
PORK STAR

Up in the outhouse, Slogg slept. He figured that he might as
well take a nap while the batter did its work, and then hobble
down again for a dinner of deep-fried pork parts. He drooled
in his slumber as he thought about it.

As Slogg's sleeping brain descended into dreamland, in
his mind's eye he saw the muddy, worm-infested fields of his
farm. He was knee-deep in the manure pile, and the grubs were
crawling over his withered flesh, slithering through the groove
in his hoof. His insides were twisted and pickled, but he felt
an unfamiliar warmth from above. This heat coming down
on his head was pleasant; unlike the jagged, flaming barbs of
the sun's rays, this heat was soft and comforting, draping over
his shoulders like a woolen pea coat. Herconium removed his
tattered straw hat and felt a gentle presence on his brow. He
dimly recalled the porcelain hand of his mother, before she ran
off with a scarecrow. He looked up to see the source of these
sweet sensations, and found that hovering above him was the
thousand-pound pig whose ears he had spared that morning.
The giant boar was gently bobbing in the blue sky, his ruddy
pink skin emanating a salmon-colored glow that radiated
towards the brown earth below.

Slogg woke with a start, confused by this mysterious
vision. He pushed it out of his mind as he made his way down
the hill. His second head was still sleeping, snoring loudly as
he hobbled towards the pen, intent on tasting the pigs' ears

that had been boiling in oil as he napped. Weaving among the swollen, earless hogs, he approached the bubbling cauldron of cooking fat and his hairy nostrils sucked up the sensual aroma of fried pork. His second head snorted loudly and woke up, exclaiming, "Sure smells good, don't it?"

Slogg's primary head responded with a nod, and reached into the steaming batter, plucking a crispy brown pig ear from the pot, ignoring the blistering boils that the scalding grease singed onto his fingers. He took a bite, then held it out to his auxiliary head to taste as well. "Mmmmm," they both hummed, gnashing the fried meat and feeling a serpentine energy spurt through their veins. The pigs' ears seemed to provoke the same unearthly sensations that the skull-toads had, which was to be expected, since the pigs had been feasting on the fallen frogs just previous to the shearing of their ears.

Head number two then turned its attention back to the black pot. "Let's have one o' them toads, too," he said, and reached for one of the skull-headed sky frogs that had by now been cooked to a golden shade. They took turns nibbling on the cooked critter's body, finally biting off its crispy, coated cadaver head as well. Slogg's blood pulsated and churned, and then with a deep shudder, he sprouted a third arm from beneath his blue denim overalls.

"That'll come in handy," said head number one, admiring his new appendage. "Time to get packing." With his new arm, he grabbed the cauldron of Slogg's Frying Batter and its bounty of golden bits of hogs and frogs, and headed back towards the outhouse. Behind him, the big boar, surrounded still by fawning rabbits and rodents, eyed the double-headed human and smiled faintly. Then he closed his eyes and the bunnies, squirrels, badgers and raccoons that formed a circle around him fell silent and sat down, their haunches in the mud and their paws folded in solemn expectation. With a crack of thunder in the cloudless blue sky, a bolt of lightning shot down above the pigpen, and when the giant hog opened his eyes, they were now three in number; a hypnotic new ocular orb resided in the middle of his massive pink forehead. The smaller animals all erupted in excited chirps and chattering, forming a woodland chorus that heralded the huge hog's final transformation.

CHAPTER 5

BOILED BOAR AND GENERAL STORE

Back up in the outhouse, Farmer Slogg was busily engaged in the pursuit of his livelihood. As a purveyor of crispy pigs' ears fried in Slogg's Famous Batter, in accordance with his family's renowned recipe, he used all three hands' thirteen fingers to transfer the fresh-cooked hog pieces out of their iron bucket and into the containers depicting dancing faeries, for them to be sold in town to connoisseurs of fine pork products.

"Let's put them toads in, too," said Slogg's second head.

"But them toads…" Farmer Slogg paused, struggling to put his thoughts into words. "They put a feller through changes."

"Double our money," replied Slogg head number two, and this logic was irrefutable. By adding in the fried skull-frogs they'd have twice as much merchandise, and since both varieties of animal were coated in a thick golden batter, the foreign ingredients wouldn't have been immediately obvious to the naked eye. Slogg shrugged and began shuffling the fried frogs into the containers as well. When the fry bucket was empty, a good two dozen boxes were full of the strange delicacies. Farmer Slogg loaded them into a red child's wagon parked beneath the willow tree behind the outhouse and rolled down the hill, jumping into the wagon to avoid the bloodthirsty worms on the ground.

Slogg's meat wagon rolled down past the pigpen and continued 'round the bend, away from Slogg's farm and onto the rural road that led into town. On occasion Slogg would drop his right leg over the side of the wagon and propel them along by kicking his hoof against the dusty road.

In due time, Slogg's wagon rolled down Mane Street of Slogg's Holler (the misspelling of "main" generations ago had achieved a state of de facto permanence). A funeral parlor, a nickelodeon, and Wallbog's General Store were the active emporiums, shouldering an abandoned doctor's office and a boarded-up brothel. The jail and mayoral office was located behind Mane Street in an alley. Slogg's hoof in the dirt halted their progress in front of Wallbog's General Mercantile, Grocery and Feed Store, and cradling the stack of containers of Slogg's Famous Battered Hogs (and frogs), he strolled inside.

"Pitchin' a double-header, Herconium?" Wallace N. Wallbog laughed at his own joke from behind the register. The spokes of a wagon wheel turned slowly overhead, serving as a makeshift cooling device. The plywood shelves were stocked primarily with cobweb-covered canisters of hair pomade and trout bait, though the local fishing hole, Slogg's Slough, had failed to produce a catch for ages.

Farmer Slogg's heads nodded in unison towards Wallbog, who was a pasty man of sizable girth, with a prominent curl of hair located in the center of his otherwise bald noggin. This lone curl was Wallbog's pride and joy; he combed and groomed it obsessively.

"Got some more pork cracklin's for ya," Slogg said, shoving the twenty-odd cardboard containers onto the counter. The insides were still hot, and brown grease the color of dung dripped and spread on the counter-top.

"Them do smell good, Herconium," Wallbog said, sticking his nose into the top box. Squinting his pupils through his bottle-cap glasses, he peered inside. "What's this?" he inquired, reaching in and pulling up one of the batter-encased frogs, its hollow eye sockets and skeletal countenance visible beneath the golden-crusted veneer. "This here ain't no ear. Is it?" Wallbog had a keen eye, the product of his many years spent as a proprietor of dry goods and imported snakeskin. Wallbog inspected the deep-fried creature, tracing the outline of its bulbous body and humanoid head. "Is it one o' them weird critters that was fallin' from the sky last night?"

"Yep."

"How's it taste?"

"Try it yore self."

Wallbog sniffed the crusty delicacy, and raised his eyebrows. With a 'here goes nothing' expression, he popped the entire mutant toad into his mouth and chewed aggressively. His eyes glazed over.

"Well?" Farmer Slogg asked from both mouths. Wallbog stared into space as if entranced. A faint rustling sound came from the top of his head as his lone lock of hair sprang to life. The curl rose up to a straight point like a unicorn horn and then began to sprout. New tendrils of thick black hair spiraled out from the center of Wallbogs' head, then wrapped together in a thick coil of rope that drooped down into the same curled position from whence it had originated, but now at three times the size and density of the original. Wallbog came back to consciousness with an air of startled surprise, and his eyes immediately crossed to the center of his head, magnetized by the magnificent new snakelet of hair. His mouth fell open. "It's good!" he proclaimed.

"Told ya," Slogg said, incorrectly. Wallbog busied himself clearing his shelves of the pomade jars, wiping them onto the floor with his arm and replacing them with the packages of Slogg's Fine Fried Hog's Ears. "I might have some more for ya later," Farmer Slogg remarked as he exited.

"I'll take all ya got," replied Wallbog, but his attention was on his forehead as he fondled the massive curl of hair, a twitching smile on his face.

SLOGG'S FAMOUS FRIED HOGs

CHAPTER 6
FAT, FREAKS AND FAMILY

Sales were brisk at Wallbog's that day, and the following morning found many a family in Slogg's Holler dining on the delicacies that had been distributed.

The cuckoo clock in the parlor of the Furbich residence at 613 Mane Street had not worked properly since its metal springs were distended by the grasping claws of the family cat, who had died in its mechanical innards in a futile attempt to kill the bird, who was never alive to begin with, and was now even less so. At seven a.m. when the hands struck the hour, a wooden door flapped open and the cuckoo dangled out of its perch, striking its beak on the minute hand. Through the open cuckoo-door, the scent of the dead cat wafted through the halls and woke the Furbich clan from their deep sleep on the second floor.

Mother Maisybelle Furbich was the first to make it down the stairs, and she began the necessary preparations for feeding her clan. After putting a kettle of hot water on the stove, she reached into the pantry for the pink box of Farmer Slogg's Boiled Boar Bits that she had picked up at Wallbog's the previous day. She took a nibble from an oily pig's ear and placed the remainder on the Lazy Susan, the rotating circular tray at the center of the table. "Come an' git it!" she shrieked.

"Mornin' Mother Maisybelle," Father Furbich said, taking his seat at the head of the table. He sniffed the caked crust of the ears on the table. "Are these from Slogg's farm?"

"Yes dear," she said, hovering over him with a steaming teakettle in her hand. "Would you like some coffee, Tom dear?" He made no reply, but stuck out his cup in her direction. She poured hot water into it, and then sprinkled in some brown powder from a porcelain container that was shaped like a big-eyed poodle. She stirred it with her index finger. Tompost Furbich was peering intently at the Lazy Susan, spinning it slowly and inspecting the ears as they rotated by. He reached over and pulled out one of the fried frogs.

The Furbich children bounded down the stairs, scratching and tangling with each other like rabid badgers. "Horphense! Elwore! Stop feudin'," Mother Maisybelle squawked, and she walloped each of them upside the head with a pair of potholders. The siblings then settled into their chairs. Little Elwore's eyes bugged from his pointy head when he saw the heap of hog's ears on the table. Without saying a word, he grabbed two and started chewing from both sides of his mouth.

"These look funny," Horphense said skeptically, before taking a bite from one of the skull-toads.

Father Furbich's eyes were rolling back in his sockets, and a wisp of purple smoke escaped from inside his starched shirt-collar. He dropped the half-eaten deep-fried amphibian into his lap. "They're quite fresh," he moaned.

Following this endorsement, the four of them dug in with gusto, spinning the serving plate at the center of the table and grabbing, munching and slurping until the Lazy Susan was empty, their stomachs were full, and their brains were buzzing with strange, unearthly energies. The plaid tablecloth appeared to be levitating from the table, forming a grid pattern in the center of the room that became a vortex at the center of the universe. And then, Tompost Furbich grew a large hunchback.

"Oh," he remarked, craning his eyes towards the fleshy mass that had erupted from behind his neck, shredding his dark grey suit.

"Cool!" Elwore exclaimed, gaping at his father. Then his own pubescent body experienced a strange transformation of its own as his nether regions swelled in a way that they never had before, and then kept swelling. The table rose in his corner.

"Oh my," said Mother Maisybelle Furbich, who was feeling a little different herself. Already a sizeable woman, she found herself being lifted up from her chair, bobbing as if bouncing on a hobbity-horse. "Oh my," she repeated, putting her hands at her sides. Her posterior had increased exponentially, creating a bountiful pair of buttocks that made for an astounding amount of ass. "Oh my," she said a third time. Meanwhile, young Horphense, who had been cackling with joy when her previously flat chest sprouted two large globes, was now silent with confusion as a third mammary stretched the woolen confines of her sweater.

An uneasy calm descended as these transformations, having reached their apex, ceased to mutate further, and the

Furbich family settled into their new physical situations. Then their stomachs began to collectively rumble. They were still hungry. "I want more pigs' ears," Horphense said.

"Yes, well that's all we have for now," Maisybelle replied, and she continued with her morning routine, giving each of the children their lunch pails and scooting them out the door to go to school. Elwore and Horphense exited eagerly, excited to show off their growth spurts to their school chums. Maisybelle brought a bag lunch to her husband, who was leering at her increased rear assets. "You look good enough to eat," he drooled. Flattered, but somewhat fearful, she put his hat on his hunchback and pointed him towards the door.

"Have a nice day at the morgue, dear. I'll see you at lunch time."

CHAPTER 7

THE SALESMAN AND THE SHANTY TRAMP'S SURPRISE

As the day wore on, Slogg's Famous Fried Hog's Ears were devoured in various quarters of Slogg's Holler, with similarly interesting results. Case in point was the experience of a traveling salesman on the outskirts of town.

Borace Telligman doffed his straw hat and spit in the brim, hoping it would cool down his sweating head. He scowled up at the noonday sun, then scowled down at the rural road he traveled on, halfway between Mane Street and Slogg's Farm, where the dirt road branched off in numerous forlorn tributaries that dead-ended at various patches of forlorn agricultural enterprises. Decaying barns covered with inscrutable hex symbols tilted over rows of turnip roots and wilting lettuce leaves. Albino goats eyed him furtively.

He lugged a battered leather suitcase, the contents of which were solely a demonstration model of the Handi-Sweep Bible Duster system, a contrivance that he had undertaken to sell to the good people of Slogg's Holler, but after two days of traveling the back roads of the backwater burg without making a single sale, he was ready to give up. The few prospective customers he'd found were suitably impressed with his wares, but could only offer mongoose eggs or porcelain hatpins as payment, not the cold hard cash that he (and the boys in the central office) required. He squinted his eyes to either side of the road, trying to discern if any of the ramshackle huts that sat on the horizon were inhabited.

Telligman's jaded eye instinctively gravitated to a small cloud of dust next to a dilapidated habitat constructed of corrugated metal and what looked like foamcore. The dust, however, was being generated by something curvy, and Telligman's heat-stricken mind filled in the gaps to form a mental picture of the one thing he desired as much as money: womankind. He lugged his suitcase off of the road and waddled furiously towards her.

The hovel was even less appealing once it was fully within eyeshot. Its windows lacked glass and the door seemed to be held on with duct tape; it stood on a large plot of land whose earth was black and foul-smelling. Rusted farm equipment littered the bleak landscape, but it seemed impossible to Telligman that anything could have grown here. "Well, one thing did grow here," Telligman corrected himself. The curvy cloud of dust that he had espied was indeed female and human, and was in no way a disappointment to Telligman. In fact, she was just what Telligman was hoping for. She was young but not too young, with enough freckles to make her face look like a plump tomato, topped off with pigtails held in place with what looked like shoelaces. She wore a homemade dress fashioned from a tablecloth and was gyrating with a hula-hoop while nibbling on a fried pig ear, oblivious to her visitor. Her eyes were crossed.

"Why hello, ma'am," Telligman said, tipping his hat to the young lady.

"Who're you?" she asked, continuing to gyrate her hoop and nibble on her ear.

"Ah, Borace Telligman's my name, miss, but you can call me Bo. And am I to presume that you are the lady of the house?"

The girl let her hoop drop and she giggled, revealing a large gap between her buck teeth. "Ma and Pa are out, if'n that's what you mean, sir. My name's Floretta," she said, giggling again, and sticking the rest of the hog's ear into her mouth so that she could extend her hand to Borace. Borace bowed down and kissed it, which made Floretta laugh again, expelling the remainder of the hog's ear out of her mouth and onto Borace's jacket.

He smiled, wiping away the grease, and said, "Well, I'd just love to show you what I have here in this suitcase. Do you think it would be alright if we ducked out of this heat for a spell?" She giggled once more and led him inside the ramshackle hutch, where the floor was covered in sawdust and the furniture was constructed of egg crates. A family of raccoons scurried into the corner as Telligman unlocked his suitcase, extracting the Handi-Sweep Bible Duster system.

"You see, you hold it by this here handle, and then you can clean your house with the Bible on the end, with the pages open to your favorite passage. As you scrub the walls or floor," he grimaced as he looked at the condition of the immediate walls and floor, which were covered with soup-spills and hornet droppings, "you're achieving a cleanliness next to Godliness."

"Oh, Bo! That's just about the most perfect thing I've ever seen!" she said, drawing out the 'r' in perfect by rolling her tongue. "Can I try?"

"Why sure, why don't you just grab it like this," Bo said, taking her by the shoulder and wrapping her arms around the handle. He leaned in behind her neck, breathing hot and fetid on her drooping shoulder. "And then you apply a little pressure…"

Floretta moaned as the Bible at the end of the stick rubbed up against her leg. With a burst of passion they dropped the duster and flung themselves onto the egg-crate table at the center of the room, displacing the box of Slogg's Famous Fried Hog Parts as they wrestled feverishly. Bo pulled at Floretta's tablecloth blouse with his teeth, exposing her bosom, which he pushed his sweaty forehead into, licking frenetically at her salty skin. The home-made dress fell to the floor.

"Hey, who dat?" barked a deep voice, all of a sudden. Bo froze and turned towards the door, expecting to see an angry husband with a gun, which had been his experience numerous times in the past. But there was no one there. Then he felt a nibbling at his pants, and he returned his attentions to Floretta. He kissed her, tasting the remains of Slogg's famous frying batter between her teeth. The nibbling sensation continued down by his fly, however, and Bo was confused. He looked down to see a face protruding from Floretta's belly. Its tongue was licking at his pants. Aside from the quivering mouth, it had an eye and a runny nose, and it was right where Floretta's belly button should be. Bo leaped back; the face continued to wag its tongue.

"Oh, that's just a lil' ol' tummy ache. The fried piggy ears brought it on, I think," Floretta giggled, patting the tumorous belly-face's forehead. Borace Telligman screamed, and he hastily ran out the front door, tearing it from its duct-taped hinges.

"Where you goin'?" the belly-face called after the flee-ing salesman. After a few min-utes, Floretta got up from the table and put her dress back on. Then she smiled and picked up the Handi-Sweep Bible Duster system that he had left behind. She cleaned the cobwebs from the walls with a page from the book of Revelations.

37

CHAPTER 8
STRANGE LOVE

At noon, Mr. Furbich headed home from the morgue. On the way, he stopped by Wallbog's Mercantile and purchased the last available box of Slogg's Famous Battered Boar Bits. "They been selling like hotcakes," Wallbog said. He had slicked his lock of hair up into something resembling a unicorn horn.

"I'm not surprised," Furbich replied. "They make a new man out of you."

"That's the truth."

Mr. Furbich hurried to his house with the cardboard container. Mother Maisybelle Furbich greeted her husband at the door. "Why Tompost Furbich, you're early for lunch! Is anything wrong?"

"Why no, mother, I just thought we might have ourselves a nice long lunch together. I got us some more ears..." Her eyes sparkled as she eyed the pink box under his armpit. They sat down at the kitchen table and started eating the oily items straight from the container. Tompost licked his lips afterwards; strange desires were overtaking him. He removed his pants.

"Why Tom! Look at you!" Maisybelle gasped. Tompost looked downward, and found that he had two protrusions where there used to be one. "Let's go up to the bedroom," she winked, heading for the stairs. "And bring the rest of our lunch, dear."

Tompost followed her up the stairs, nibbling on a fried sky-frog along the way. By the time he reached the mattress,

38

his hunchback was quivering, seeping a gelatinous fluid from its pores. Maisybelle shed her matronly undergarments and possessed by an unusual hunger, began licking at the towering mass protruding from her husband's back. Meanwhile, Tompost Furbich was maneuvering his newfound appendages into any orifice he could find on his wife's anatomy; the selection was surprisingly numerous.

"Oh dear, I don't think you've put anything in there before," she said, moaning.

"I don't think there was ever a there before to put things in," he said oddly, sweating as he contorted into the unusual position required by this erotic endeavor. "You seem to be sprouting more holes than a golf course, my sweet."

"Oooooh," Maisybelle swooned, reaching for another hog's ear. Her flushed cheeks chewed as Mr. Furbich huffed and pushed. Their bodies were swelling, making noises like a hot dog in an oven as they plumped into new shapes. They switched positions, as Mother Furbich grew a mouth on her elbow with which she swallowed the second of Tompost's two posts, approximating a lovemaking technique that would be considered a number one hundred and thirty-eight when compared to the traditional sixty-nine.

Finding that he had an extra hand growing from a hairy patch on his shin, he grabbed at his wife's heaving breasts, of which there were now too many to count. "Yes, touch me there!" she moaned. He was chewing on a frog-leg, straining to achieve a climax to his excitement, and in doing so found that he was sprouting more and more fingers, which spread like tentacles over Maisybelle's sweaty surfaces. "Yes, and there! And there! Yes!" she screamed.

After about twenty minutes of such pornographic improvisations, and the ingestion of the remaining snacks from Slogg's farm, the couple was nearly unrecognizable. They had both become round and craterous, pounding against each other like colliding moons. "I think I'm going to express my love!"

Tompost Furbich yelled into Maisybelle's several ears. Her face had blossomed into something resembling a sunflower.

"Yes Tom," she choked, and then in a ghastly shower of passion both of them exploded into an eruption of thick fluids, their monstrous bodies soaked in a multicolored shower of slime. When it was over, they lay in a remarkable stain upon their soiled mattress on their broken bed, smoking six cigarettes out of the multitude of openings that had grown on their rotund, mutated flesh.

CHAPTER 9
HOGAPOCALYPSE

It had been three days since the strange rains came, and Slogg's two heads were discussing the future.

"We should fry the rest of these pigs," said Slogg's second head.

"But we already cut off all them ears, and none of 'em growed back," replied the original Farmer Slogg.

"That's why we got to cook up the rest of 'em, snouts and all. Wallbog prob'ly sold all the boxes we brung already." Slogg #2 reached for Daisy, the knife, which was dangling as usual from their pants-rope. Slogg #1 had control of the right arm, but the new Slogg-head had gotten pretty handy with the left. Slogg #1 surveyed the dozen huge, earless swine that were crammed into the once-spacious pigpen. Then his eyes fell on the giant boar, who despite the cramped conditions had nearly a third of the pen to himself, as his muddy brethren had given him a wide berth.

"Dang, that pig got even huger…" Farmer Slogg mused. Indeed, the big pig had swelled to two thousand pounds by now, a mighty tower of ham rising out of the sludge. As if understanding that he was being spoken of, the giant pig opened his third eye and stared right at Slogg. The eye was unblinking, and held Slogg hypnotically in its steely black gaze. Then, from the clear blue sky, a single skull-headed frog fell from above. The great pig raised his snout slightly and caught the falling frog in his mouth, all the while keeping his three eyes on Farmer Slogg. "Must be 'bout a ton, now," Slogg mused in a far-away voice. The second Slogg-head paid him no mind, as his attention was focused on testing the sharpness of Daisy's jagged edge on the tip of his finger.

"Awlright," Slogg #2 said to Slogg #1, "I'm gonna git down to bizness." He pointed Daisy towards one of the hogs.

"Let's not kill the big one," Slogg #1 said, surprising himself.

Slogg #2 gave his other head a sideways glance. "If'n you say so," he replied, spitting a wad of tobacco down into the mulch by the cloven hoof they shared. Then he raised Daisy with his left hand and began sticking her into the pigs.

The original Farmer Slogg's head experienced an unusual displeasure at the familiar sound of hogs being slaughtered, and closed his eyes, resting his head on his knobby shoulder as the left side of his body went to work. Soon he grew lethargic. It felt like his internal fluids had been replaced with bacon fat, and his blood moved slowly through clogged arteries, not making it up to his brain, which soon turned off like an unplugged toaster. The giant pig in the corner also closed his third eye and appeared to sleep as well.

Slogg #2 went methodically about his business of offing the hogs, jabbing Daisy into the fleshy pink piles of pigs, dragging the sleeping half of his body with him as he did so. Slogg #1 was oblivious to the oinks and squeals emanating from the killing floor, and in his slumber began to dream again… He dreamt that he was a worm in the earth. His wormy head was poking out of a hole in the ground, and he could feel that his slimy, cylindrical body extended for a great distance behind him. He looked to either side and saw hundreds of other worm-people sticking out of the ground, similar to himself. He could sense from the way they all moved together that they were connected deep inside the ground, like branches coming from a single stem. As Slogg slithered slightly forward, the other heads receded, and vice versa; they were like a huge coil of tangled rubber bands, spread beneath the surface of the planet. Up above them all, the great hog hovered in the sky, much as he had in Slogg's previous dream. But the boar was different this time; whereas before he had simply radiated warmth like the sun, this time his third eye was open, staring intently down at Slogg and all the other little half-worms. The giant pig's mouth opened, making a great sucking sound as he began to inhale the air around him, and the very atmosphere of the planet as well.

Slogg and the other human-headed worms were pulled out of the ground towards the hog's siphoning maw, pulled towards the open, pink mouth, as gleaming tusks slowly protruded from the oral chasm. The worm-folks' bodies became thin as they were stretched forward through the sky. This was uncomfortable, since all of them were attached at the center of the earth, their ends being tied together down deep below. As their heads were pulled upwards towards the gaping teeth of the giant pig in the sky, it seemed inevitable that Slogg and the others would eventually snap in half.

CHAPTER 10
A BAGFUL O' BACKBEAT

Back in town, country-western singer Churlotta Lovelorn was finding that her muse had deserted her. She sat on her porch, plucking a banjo made from a rotted tree limb with the sinewy ligaments of a stray cat stretched across its surface. She plucked at them with her long, curled nails, a deep twang emitting from the frying pan that was attached to the gnarled branch. Over this rural melody, she attempted to vocalize:

"Nobody to churn my butter, no man to milk my udders
Got a plowed field that won't yield and a window with no shutters."

The raccoon sitting on the porch next to her howled in pain. Churlotta sighed and wrinkled her forehead. "Maybe I'll try writin' a gospel number," she said to the raccoon, who nodded his masked eyes. With her fingers twitching against the catguts again, she chirped out another syrupy sonnet:

"Well, the Devil is your manager in this boxing ring called life
And he'll tell you to take a dive when the third bell strikes
But are you gonna stand your ground or simply hit the floor
From the thunderin' fists o' the Lord?"

The raccoon scurried away, and Churlotta threw the banjo down in disgust.

"Hey Churlotta, sorry we're late." The huge figure of Dormutt, the bassist in Churlotta's band, filled the dirt path that led to Churlotta's porch. He lugged with him a stand-up bass guitar that was crudely fashioned from the hollow log of an old oak tree. Close behind Dormutt was the scrawny figure of Fuzzy, the drummer of the trio. Fuzzy carried a snare drum under his arm and held a plastic bag of greenish fluid in his hand. "We stopped by Horlope's place," Dormutt continued.

Churlotta snorted and gave her tangled red hair a shake; she knew that a visit to Horlope's meant that her rhythm section would be blind on moonshine by sundown.

She squinted at the gallon bag of green liquid. "There's critters in it?"

"Well, it was the darnedest thing," Dormutt said, sitting down on the porch next to Churlotta and shifting his bass into a music-playing position. "Fuzzy and I popped over 'round noon, and Horlope was nowhere to be found. Neither was Phendle or Cousin Kerth, and they're usually all hangin' round 'bout that time of day – but their still had a full tub o' shine in it." He grinned crookedly at Churlotta.

"So you two done helped yourselves, hmmm?" She winked.

"We'll pay him later," Fuzzy stammered. He was a wiry, nervous fellow, whose Adam's apple bounced like a ping-pong ball while he talked. He opened up the plastic bag and stuck his small nose into the acidic potion. His nostrils brushed against one of the skull-headed frogs floating in the briny alcohol. "Pheeuw," he exclaimed, inhaling half the bag into his head. Then, shaking even more than usual, he perched his snare drum on his knee and pulled a pair of chopsticks from the pocket of his overalls. Playing with Chinese eating utensils was a hallmark of Fuzzy's percussion style.

Dormutt began slapping his beefy paw against the strings of his log-bass. "You write any new songs, Churlotta?" he asked the leader of the band.

"Naw," she replied, looking forlornly down the dirt path to the flatlands beyond. "I tried, but nothing good came."

Dormutt nodded. "Shucks, don't let it fret you none. You'll git somethin' writ event-chully." He fiddled around in his trousers, pulling out something pink and greasy. "Care for a pig's ear?"

Churlotta shook her head again. She picked up her banjo. "No thanks, I gots to watch my figure. Show bizness, y'know." Dormutt popped the pig part in his mouth and joined Churlotta in playing a simple country rhythm in the approximate key of E. His hollow log resonated as he pulled at the chicken wire strung across its length, producing a low, loping sound. Churlotta's frying-pan banjo plucks harmonized with a scratchy jangle and Fuzzy joined in with a clang against his snare drum, which was fashioned from a spittoon with a tangle of barbed wire strung over its lip. Churlotta hummed melodiously over the instruments as their rudimentary song lilted up from the fields and hovered with the whippoorwills in the summer sunshine. Suddenly, Fuzzy executed a drum roll with a flourish of musicality significantly outside the realm of his usual expertise. Dormutt and Churlotta looked over in surprise, and saw that Fuzzy was employing a newly grown third arm, which added considerable augmentation to his drumming style.

"That's cheating," Churlotta admonished.

CHAPTER 11

POINTY-TOOTHED PROTECTORATE OF THE PEOPLE

The Honorable Mayor Tiligree Beronius Phigg, or T. B. as he was called by his cronies, liked to describe himself as a self-made man. His mother, a waitress and a drifter, discarded him into Slogg's Swamp when she first saw his puffy, sniveling face. The infant Phigg was perfectly happy in the murky bog into which he was deposited, and lived on a diet of slugs and lilies until curiosity led him to shore, where he ingratiated himself into a family of rats. It was there that he acquired the social graces that he would come to employ as a politician.

T. B. Phigg began his illustrious career of public service as the Slogg's Holler dogcatcher, one of two elected positions in the small town (the other being the mayoral one, which at the time was held by one Gerratard Grotense). Slogg's Holler prided itself on being engaged in the political process, and as such nearly the whole town turned out for the debate that was held on Mane Street one summer afternoon following the fly-paper auction. Phigg's competition for the title of town dogcatcher stood on a pickle barrel and made wild proclamations of integrity and hard-working-ness, punctuated by swoops of his dog-catching net, which he carried with experience, as he was the incumbent. When it came time for Phigg to make a statement, he stood up upon the pickle barrel and simply opened his mouth.

Years of living with a family of rats as an impressionable youth had rubbed off on Phigg in a profound way, and as he bared his teeth the townsfolk gasped – he had four massively long and sharp teeth, two incisors and two molars, that he bared at the crowd and then at his opponent, hissing. The people were impressed, as aggression was the characteristic they valued most in a dogcatcher, and Phigg was elected handily.

The relationship between Phigg and his superior, Mayor Gerratard Grotense, was not without its tensions. It turned out that Slogg's Holler had no stray dogs, as they had all been eaten long ago by the rambunctious raccoons that infested the fields and ditches (and some of which were adopted as pets by the locals). With no prey to chase and trap, Phigg decided instead to stuff Mayor Grotense into the empty cage in the back of his wagon and drive him out of town. When he returned, he assumed the office of Mayor of Slogg's Holler, as he was the logical successor.

The civic center of Slogg's Holler was located in an alley off of Mane Street that housed the town jail, its postal office (which employed a fleet of trained and rather bored pigeons) and the offices of the mayor, which Phigg had decorated with an abundance of patriotic bunting. The Stars and Stripes drooped from every corner of the small room. He had taken Old Glory from the town's flagpoles and tacked it against the windows and used it as a rug, so that when entering the mayoral chamber one had the sensation of being in the absolute heart of the country. On this particular day, Phigg was sleeping behind his desk, drooling on the star that represented the 31st state.

There was a knock upon the door, which Phigg struggled to ignore, but to the persistence of which he eventually gave in. "Who's there!" he barked.

"It's Dorp."

Phigg sighed. Dorp was the town deputy and notary public, and Phigg's only employee in running the governmental functions of Slogg's Holler. "Get yer ass in," Phigg barked, wiping spittle from his drooping moustache, which had never been trimmed in all his years since leaving his mother rat.

"I'm back from tax collectin'," Dorp said depressedly. He was a gangly simpleton, almost eight feet tall but only a foot and a half wide, as if he was once a normal man but had been stretched on the rack. He reached into his pocket and deposited two buttons, an Indian nickel and a piece of lint on Phigg's desk.

"That's all you could get?" Phigg sputtered, disgusted. He opened a lead safe behind the flag at his back and deposited this pitiful collection into its empty confines.

"Well, I got this too," Dorp said, exiting briefly through the door. When he returned he was dragging a misshapen man who was chewing on a human leg, not his own.

Phigg got up and walked over to take a closer look. The young man on the floor was grossly mutated, with a head that resembled a birdcage and an odd number of eyes. He was chewing on the toenails of the detached body part. "Where'd ya find him?" Phigg asked Dorp.

"In town. It's the Cragmire kid. I was making my rounds, and when I came to the Cragmire place there was no answer, so I let myself in and I found him just like this. I think the foot might've belonged to his sister."

"Did you find the sister?"

"Nope. He must've eated her, T.B."

"Well, put him in the lockup," Phigg instructed, and then he sat down behind his desk and watched as Dorp pulled the body out the door, still chewing...

CHAPTER 12
CAREWORN CATHEDRAL

As the sins of lust and gluttony ran rampant in the slimy bowels of Slogg's Holler, Sunday services at the town church were slimly attended. The structure housing the ministry of Reverend Horel Burnbroom had once been a barn, a history appropriate to this particular Sunday's mass, as the only parishioners in attendance were a goat and two chickens (and the goat had only come to lick the holy water). The size of his ministry did not deter the fervor of good Reverend Burnbroom, however. He stood behind a pulpit constructed of egg crates and shingling, ranting loudly towards the rooftop.

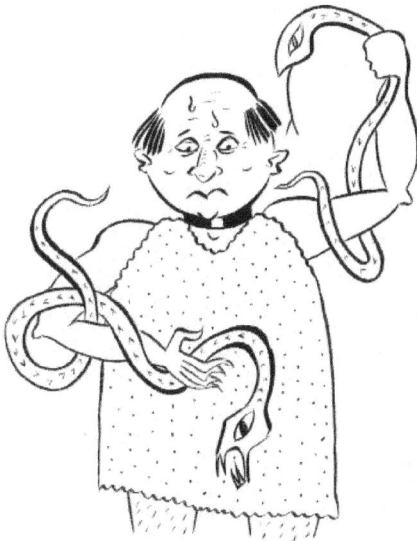

"No greater fury hath the eternal spirit than when spurned by the venomous stupidities of the blunderhood of man!" The hex symbol that had originally adorned the lofty heights of the barn remained, and its pentagram design cast a pagan shadow on the proceedings, an irony unnoticed by Brother Burnbroom, who had no formal training, belonged to no established order, and had only his own vague notions of religious traditions to employ. Thusly, he was free to improvise his own sacraments in accordance with whatever mystical wisps of ceremonious intent happened to grace his fevered mind. It was in this spirit that he kept the top of his head shaved like a monk, and wore an empty potato sack as a shirt, since its brown billowing resembled a robe to Burnbroom. Today he was set to employ a program of speaking in tongues and the handling of snakes, techniques that he had learned of in overheard conversations and which Burnbroom hoped would bring him increased patronage and a swelling of his congregation.

"Hagglabagglabar!" Burnbroom frothed, his tongue wagging wildly between purple lips. He pulled two snakes from a breadbasket beneath the pulpit and dangled them from each hand. He wrapped them around his neck. As green scales slithered under his cardboard collar, his eyes crossed and he increased his poetical expressions. "Florraragulabinoristat!" he gurgled, and in so doing, startled the reptile on his left side, which bit him on the elbow and then squirmed out the door, scaring away the two chickens in the process. Depressed at the loss of two-thirds of his audience, Burnbroom sank to his knees. Then the second snake, which had wrapped itself around his torso, bit him on the pecker.

"Choohoorabillfoogesh!" he moaned.

CHAPTER 13
LURE OF THE LARD

Even though he had a second head growing out of his neck, Farmer Slogg was feeling lonely. He was not a sentimental man by nature; when his mother ran off with a scarecrow, he didn't notice until the crops were eaten by crows. When his siblings disappeared into the creek, he thought of scrounging amongst the creek-bed for their shoes, until he remembered that they had none. Nevertheless, now that twelve of his thirteen pigs were off to market, and there was nothing but their poop remaining, a vague unease crept upon him. "Think I'll go check on the last pig," he remarked, rousing himself from the floor of the outhouse.

He was unable to move, however. Now that his second head had gained control over half of his body, a subtle battle of wills had started to sprout within the divided form of Farmer

Slogg. The original Farmer Slogg, Slogg #1, craned his neck to face his mutant twin, whose eyes were closed. "Getting' up now," Slogg #1 said.

"I'm sleepin," replied Slogg #2, eyes still shut. Slogg #1 muttered to himself, and after a moment's frustrated deliberation, decided to haul himself out of the outhouse even if he had to drag the other half of him behind forcibly. To that end, Slogg #1 dug his fingernails into the outhouse door, unstuck himself from the wall and struggled towards the world outside. Unfortunately, Slogg's second and most uncooperative head had control of the left side of Slogg's body, which meant that the original Farmer Slogg had only his hoof to work with as far as lower mobility went. As the second Slogg remained asleep in protest, Slogg #1 dragged himself down the hill as well as he could, lurching willy-nilly amongst the grubs and bloodworms, towards the pigpen below.

A hundred years ago, this trip from outhouse to pigpen was much shorter; in fact, the pigpen was situated directly below the outhouse, and the pigs would dine on the offal produced in the toilets above. This method of disposal is still utilized in the Indian state of Goa, but as lackadaisical as the community of Slogg's Holler was, this economical procedure was found too unhygienic for the local consumers of Slogg's Boiled Hog Parts.

The lone pig in Slogg's pen was big enough to fill its confines easily; the giant hog was two thousand pounds or so of mountainous mammal. Of the two billion pigs alive on the planet Earth, this swine, warty and triple-eyed, was surely King. Farmer Slogg sat down in front of the massive animal, and the hog's third eye winked at him.

Slogg's second head woke with a grumble and spat. "What we doin' down here? We gone finally kill this one now?" He started to reach for Daisy, but Slogg #1 had shifted the knife over to his side of the body while the other slept, to keep it out of his brother's reach. After a half-hearted grasping around,

Slogg #2 snorted and gave up. "Fine, keep yer damn pig," he said, and he went back to sleep.

Farmer Slogg sat and stared at the giant hog for a while, and the huge boar looked back at him. Then a rustling sound was heard behind them, and an unlatching of the pigpen gate. Slogg swiveled his head, and saw that one of the townsfolk had come trespassing on Slogg's Farm, which was unusual – Farmer Slogg rarely had visitors. It was a middle-aged man in a checkered suit; Slogg had seen him on Mane Street now and then. He had large boils and pustules sprouting from his skin now, as well as massive growths on his torso that stretched the polyester fabric of his coat. Slogg looked at him inquisitively.

"I come to see the pig," he replied succinctly, standing a yard distant. Slogg was immobile for a moment, but then gave him an understanding nod. The suited gentleman took a seat next to Slogg and they both faced the great pig, which gazed back at them with a solemn expression. A purple spiral slowly emerged in the black pupil of the pig's third eye, and rotated. Then the pig belched, and the deep rumbling sound echoed into the brains of the two mutant men, reverberating through their synapses and filling them with heavy vibrations.

CHAPTER 14
SONG OF THE INBRED ANGEL

After band practice was over, Churlotta foraged in her yard for dinner. She gathered up some dandelion thistles and kudzu vines that drooped from the poplar trees and boiled them in a black kettle in her kitchen. Her preference for dining on found vegetation rather than the greasy meats favored by the rest of the townsfolk had begun as an attempt to stay slim for the spotlight. Churlotta had ambitions to make her way to the top of the music industry, to one day live in Tennessee and host her own talk show, where she would sing her questions to her guests in a studio fashioned with green shag carpeting and leopard-print drapes. Over time, however, she came to genuinely acquire a taste for the snakeflower roots and jimsonweeds that sprouted from the craggy dirt of Slogg's Holler. Now when she saw the gristly flesh being masticated in the gaping jaws of the others, their skin pink and oily like the pig bits they gulped with abandon, she was filled with disgust. She kept this notion to herself, however.

A tornado had taken out the west-facing wall of her small house, so as she fell asleep in the hammock that she had strung from the chimney mantle to the closet-door knob, she gazed out at the big yellow moon that shone down on the creeping things of the night, as owls hooted plaintively in concert with the crickets' crooked chirping. She drifted off to slumber with her frying-pan banjo held in her hands, gently strumming along with the soft sounds of the endless countryside that was her fourth wall.

Behind the veil of sleep, Churlotta's nocturnal notions pictured her strolling through the crabgrass in a nightgown, meandering in the silent meadows of her mind's eye. Her dream-self stooped down to smell a bloom of belladonna, and as the florid scent of deadly nightshade filled her nostrils she began to hear the faint sound of singing in the distance. She raised her head to seek out its source, and saw a jackrabbit bounding across the field and disappearing over the slope. Churlotta followed, floating across the pasture as a warm breeze buoyed her forward.

She came to the edge of the field, where the ground descended sharply into a great valley. She could make out shadows in the darkness below, shifting in circles and chanting – here was the source of the soft singing she had heard. She sat down to watch them, mesmerized by their rhythmic motions and gentle incantations. Gradually, a pale pink light began to dawn on the figures down in the valley – it was a cluster of people, nude save for beads and feathers that adorned their skin, twirling their arms and spiraling around each other in an entranced fashion. Their heads were tilted toward the sky as they mouthed their odd song, but they were not looking towards Churlotta; they were looking above her, and she tilted her neck to follow their gaze.

What she saw above her was the giant figure of Slogg's Hog, radiating warmth and magnificence as the third eye in the middle of his forehead opened to reveal a smiley face, the yellow circle and black lines of which reminded Churlotta of her childhood and the buttons that once emblazoned her jean jacket. Honeybees buzzed about her tangle of red hair and she lay in the morning grass, feeling the heat of the great sun-pig that hung overhead in the dawn, and listening to the dancers' passionate warbling of praise and jangling of beads. She looked downwards again and saw that the circle of gentle freaks frolicking below now had the heads of pigs, not people. She lay back in the dew as the bees pollinated her scalp, basking in the beatification of the ham-filled heavens above; she then closed her eyes and fell asleep within her dream.

When Churlotta awoke the next morning, she had no memory of her night voyage, but found that she was humming a strange song on her lips. As she unrolled from the hammock and stared at the blue sky that abutted her half-home, the melody persisted in her mind. Excitedly, she fingered her banjo and with little effort, began to sing...

"There's a hog up in heaven who's a hunnerd miles wide
And you won't eat his bacon 'cuz his skin is full of eyes"

CHAPTER 15
POLITICS WITHOUT PANTS

After Dorp removed the mutated murderer from his midst, Mayor Phigg spent the rest of the afternoon satisfying his constituency. In particular, he was satisfying a constituent by the name of Mrs. Enid Bountiface, who had come to the honorable Mayor in the hopes of gaining approval for a proposed 12-foot extension to her wig farm, which had heretofore sprouted no hairpieces. Enid was hopeful, however; this hopefulness was encouraged by Mayor Phigg, who was proposing his own six-inch extension into her flesh farm, an offer that Mrs. Enid Bountiface was only half-resisting.

"Now T.B., you behave yourself," she giggled, slapping away the bristly fingers that groped at her drooping bosom.

Mayor Phigg snorted through his abundant moustache and reached for his liquor cabinet. "How about a lil' toot to warm up the afternoon," he said smoothly as he reached for a glass flower vase full of fluid. He grabbed a couple of paper cups from his wastebasket and squatted down next to Mrs. Bountiface, who was sitting in the visitor's chair next to Phigg's desk.

Enid peered into the vase. "Why, there's frogs in it!" she grimaced, wrinkling her nose.

Phigg eyed the vase, and saw that this was so. As part of Dorp's tax-collecting rounds, the deputy had paid a visit to Horlope Charlip, and finding the man missing, had siphoned off a gallon or two from the still out back and brought it in as a government collection. Phigg, ever the skillful politician, was

61

quick to pacify his guest's concern. "Why, that's the latest thing – it's a French recipe."

"Ooooh, French!" Enid gasped, and she downed her cup of the green fluid. Phigg smiled and did the same. Then, brushing the cups from the table, he attempted to reposition Mrs. Bountiface onto the surface of his desk, draping her limbs over the American flag that served as his ink-blotter. Enid was distracted by the effects of the mysterious moonshine, however, and fell to the floor. "Oooh, French!" she repeated, burping up scales. Her eyes rotated slowly as her face, already rouged red with makeup, began to grow even more flushed, eventually ripening to the rich hue of a pomegranate.

As the alcohol and its taste of torrential toad-rain filled Phigg's cranium with cravings, he unzipped his trousers and felt all his blood rush to his swollen, snake-like member, which was writhing and twisting as if crawling through underbrush. He stopped his advancement towards the crumpled, swooning woman and stared in amazement as his appendage tied itself in a sailor's knot. Phigg was about to undo this phallic tangle, when he heard Deputy Dorp scream from down the hall.

"Pardon me, my dear," he said to the unconscious woman, who was swelling up like a big red blimp. He headed to the jail cell, where he found that their newly-incarcerated visitor had taken a large bite from Dorp's elbow. Dorp was standing outside the cell, holding a tray of bread and water – evidently he was just about to feed the prisoner, when the prisoner fed himself.

"Cragmire, what in the name of God's Green Earth are you doing? Dorp can't taste good at all," Mayor Phigg admonished.

The Cragmire kid looked ashamed and sheepish. "Have you got any pig's ears, T.B.?" he asked. Dorp was inspecting his arm, which was now missing a piece.

Mayor Phigg just stared at their hungry prisoner and thought to himself, "Pig's ears? Elbow biting? Something is afoot here…"

CHAPTER 16
THE MEAT OF THE MYSTERIES

The good Reverend Burnbroom stood naked at midnight, covered in kitchen utensils and screaming at a wooden door. "Gaaaah! Demons! Deliver me!" he gasped, twisting a fork into his bellybutton as his corpulent folds of flab flooded with sweat. Reverend Burnbroom was in the muddy basement of his church-barn, which was essentially a large pit dug by the former tenants of the land, a gang of criminals who passed through Slogg's Holler three decades before, and had dug the hole to hide a fortune in stolen banknotes. One morning the entire gang was pecked to death by barn-swallows, and their blood money went undiscovered until Burnbroom stumbled upon the trap door while crawling on the ground like a snake in order to better understand the motives of the serpent in the garden of Eden. When he

64

found the money, he used it to purchase a series of billboards that prophesied the end of the world as coming next week. His costly mistake was to list the actual date of the impending apocalypse, which obligated Burnbroom to purchase and erect a new sign each week to correct the date, as each week passed without the promised catastrophe, requiring an expensive postponement and revision of the world's expiration date.

In this dark moment down in the hole of Burnbroom's basement, the Reverend was desperately seeking divine inspiration. Earlier in the day he had noticed that the wood grain of his front door was full of faces, which he figured to be the work of either Jesus or Satan. In an effort to find out which, he had dragged the door from its hinges and brought it down to this pit. For good measure, he applied sharp implements of penance to his person in order to atone for his sins in this fleshly realm – rusted spoons were affixed in uncomfortable ways with electrical tape, inserted into the cavities of his corpulence and drew beads of blood as he beat his body against the dirt walls of his subterranean chamber. "Devils, why do you torment me?" he screamed at the melting faces in the oak panels of the wooden door. The faces stared back impassively. In an effort to get them to talk, he pushed a butter knife against his private parts, forcing secretions to ooze from engorged veins. Still, there was no reaction from the heads on the door. "Speak, damn you!" he cried in desperation. Then he bent to his knees, ramming a spatula into his ear canal, and in sad hope put his hands upwards together. "Maybe you're angels," he whispered. "Oh sweet heavenly ambassadors, talk to me with your feathery tongues and instruct me in my earthly mission. I am here to do your bidding!" he pleaded expectantly, but as the minutes passed in quiet darkness without incident, Burnbroom grew angry and depressed.

"Well, to Hell with y'all," he spat, and cast off the forks and spoons and electrical tape. He put a hand over the cusp of the pit and pulled himself upwards, back to the ground floor of the church. It had been another in a long series of failed attempts at experiencing a religious revelation. He had been trying for years, but had yet to receive a genuine vision of a spiritual nature. Never had a saint floated towards him by a cliff, nor had the Devil rapped on his windowpane. The carpenter from Nazareth had not even singed His holy image onto a piece of Burnbroom's toast at breakfast. As a self-proclaimed man of the cloth, it was a great embarrassment to him that he had never had any firm contact with the world beyond. But in the midst of this dejection, the slippery slope would soon work a muddy magic upon him – for Reverend Burnbroom had lost his grip at the top of the pit, and as his feet fell from the top lip of the hole, the naked man tumbled backwards onto the basement floor, striking his head against an egg-beater. Looking up in agony, Burnbroom saw a star… and something more. It was a great round shape, blurry at first but then coming into clear, pink focus. A giant pig was hovering over Reverend Burnbroom, and it opened its mouth to speak.

CHAPTER 17
TWO HEADS ARE LESSER THAN ONE

When the second Farmer Slogg head woke up, it found itself still in the pigpen, his twin head staring blankly towards the giant hog. "What th' hell, brother? You a pig lover?"

"Shut yer trap, I'm listenin'" replied the original Slogg head in an angry whisper.

Slogg #2 paused and perked up his hairy ears, but all he

heard was the grumbling sound in his own stomach. "Listenin' to whut? I don't hear nothin'."

Slogg #1 sighed. "Listenin' to the pig, you idjut. He talks through yer mind."

The second Slogg snorted. "So now you got religion, huh?" The skeptical mutant looked over at the giant hog, who was squatted down in his own excrement (being two thousand pounds, there was plenty of it) and whose third eye with its glowing spiral pupil was rotating hypnotically. Slogg #2 quickly looked away from the mesmerizing orb, and his eyes landed on the middle-aged man with the checkered suit, who was also hunkered down in the mud. The man's eyes were closed and his hands were moving in rhapsodic twirls. "And who's this freak?" Slogg #2 asked, which was ironic, coming from a cracked-headed twin growing out of the side of a neck.

"A fellow follower," Slogg #1 replied, closing his eyes to resume his meditation of telepathic reception.

"Goddamn, that does it! I'm a-gonna eat him!" Slogg #2 spat, boiling over with frustration at the idiocy of the situation. He engorged with blood, swelling up like a bruise, and grabbed willy-nilly for Daisy, the serrated knife – but Slogg #1 kept it safely out of reach on his side of the body, and held his ground resolutely, refusing to budge. Slogg #2 stewed in his juices for a moment, and then resorted to violence. Straining his half of their shared neck, he reared back his head and smashed his forehead into the skull of his twin.

Slogg #1 received the crushing blow without opening his eyes, nor uttering a sound. His forehead betrayed a visible concussion where his twin had impacted his noggin, but he showed no sign of discomfort. Slogg #2 stared at his impassive brother, confused. Then Slogg #1 said serenely, "Pork Power Prohibits Pain."

Bewildered and angry, and with his head smarting from his share of the blow, Slogg #2 took a moment more to re-evaluate his circumstances, and then a low-watt light bulb glimmered dimly above his head as he received his first good idea. He leaned towards the man in the checkered suit and barked at him. The man paused the twirling of his limbs and stared back quizzically. "Hey, checkered suit! Get yer hiney over here!" Slogg #2 yelled. The middle-aged man with the face full of boils extracted himself from his complicated yoga position, and once his legs were un-knotted, he strolled over to the two-headed farmer, his pant-bottoms brown and dripping with mud and pig poop. He raised his eyebrows towards Slogg #2.

"Yer sittin' on my farm here, and that's our hog, so you gonna have to pay me a dollar," said the enterprising second Slogg.

"Property's Properly Pigs'," the man replied enigmatically, and he handed the angry head his wallet. Slogg #2 smiled wide, his black teeth absorbing the light of the day.

CHAPTER 18
THE CRAFTY GRANNIES' KNIT AND VOMIT SOCIAL GATHERIN'

As afternoon spread an orange haze over Slogg's Holler, a twinge of excitement hovered in the air like a parasitic insect. At six o' clock the Daughters of the Lost Cause were having their seasonal quilting bee and rhubarb bake, with entertainment to be provided by Churlotta Lovelorn and Her Yodelin' Frogbottoms.

The Daughters of the Lost Cause were a gaggle of elderly matrons who appointed themselves as custodians of the rich

historical and cultural heritage of the Slogg's Holler region, but as this social order was composed of the most aged of the county's ladies, all the members suffered from degrees of dementia that rendered their knowledge of their own names a difficulty, let alone the events of preceding generations. Nevertheless, their gatherings were lively affairs, and on this occasion there were a bakers' dozen of the Daughters in attendance at the town home of Grimelda Futzwig, a nonagenarian and pillar of the community. She was vomiting blueberry pie onto a ball of yarn.

The other crones followed suit; Mrs. Pudweena Harff removed her dentures, and after nestling them in her bluish-grey hair, sucked up two bulging cheeks full of apple crumble, which she sprayed downwards as she crocheted. The ladies were jointly knitting a large quilt, as was their want. The yarn they utilized was of a singular color of yak thread that they had shorn from poor Koreb the Yak, whom they kept chained to the drainpipe. In the interests of coloration they baked a feast of pies and covered their collaborative sewing material in a drizzle of vibrant fruit-derived vomit and drool, which stained the resultant fabric in a rainbow of hues. Meanwhile, whatever menfolk and offspring were in attendance sat outside, eating the crusts and listening to country-western entertainment.

Churlotta Lovelorn was wearing a dress made especially for her at last season's quilting-bee pie-bake of the Daughters of the Lost Cause. It was a bright yellow, the result of the mastication and regurgitation of an entire grove of lemon pies. She strummed her frying pan and swayed her narrow hips as Dormutt and Fuzzy provided able backup on their log bass and spittoon drum. Her rhythm section's hearty consumption of the leftover moonshine from the Charlip still had resulted in significant growth of their musicianship. They each had four arms and four legs now, and their spidery notes ventured into areas of freeform jazz improvisation.

"I'm gonna play y'all a new song now. It came to me in a

dream, and I sure hope y'all like it," Churlotta said from the fallen barn door that served as a stage. She counted a 1-2-3-4 to her humanoid-arachnid orchestra, and then launched into her new lyrical direction:

"The pink belly bounces
A spiral eye pronounces
Where the fields are fallow we shall follow
We will grovel, we will wallow
Like a big pig's behind
Life is a pork rind"

Their small audience of senile old men (and a handful of their spawn) suddenly hopped up from their seats in the dirt and began to dance, lurching spasmodically and twirling their arms in weird windmill motions. The attendees had been lunching on a picnic of Slogg's Boiled Pork Products earlier, so they also sported additional legs with which to dance and additional heads with which to nod and bob. Churlotta looked out in wonder at such an enthusiastic reception, which her music had never before received.

After the performance was over, the rapturous audience crowded around them and pestered the trio for autographs. Churlotta and her Yodelin' Frogbottoms graciously complied, scrawling large X's on paper towels with charcoal from the barbeque grill. Once the adulators had dispersed, drummer Fuzzy went off in the tall grass with Grimelda Futzwig, who was particularly moved by the sound of his rhythmic banging. Picking up his hollow-log bass, Dormutt inquired, "When we gone play again, Churlotta?

"I was thinking we might have us a big concert over in the field at Slogg's Farm come Sunday," was her reply, which surprised them both.

CHAPTER 19

SKILLFUL MACHINATIONS OF THE CANNIBAL LOBBYIST

The next day, Mayor Phigg entertained the County Commissioner that oversaw the township of Slogg's Holler and its surrounding neighbors. "Beauroneaux, I'm glad you saw fit to come all the way on out here on such short notice," Phigg said loquaciously, extending a sweaty palm to the nervous-looking man in the gray suit and pencil-thin tie. Phigg sized up his guest, who as his immediate supervisor in the counties' political ladder, inhabited a rung that Phigg would soon like to claw his way onto. Beauroneaux Vollumineaux had inherited the position from his father, and having the pasty complexion of a Northerner, was visibly uncomfortable in the sweltering, claustrophobic confines of Phigg's flag-swathed sepulcher of a mayoral headquarters.

"Er, so you were saying... You have some sort of emergency here?" Beauroneaux inquired, fiddling with his tie and fanning himself.

"Oh yes, a dire situation. An outbreak of extreme monsterism," Phigg replied, staring intently at the County Commissioner and baring his rat teeth slightly.

"Um... Could you be more specific?"

"Dorp! Bring out the Cragmire boy!" Phigg barked, and moments later Deputy Dorp came into the office, dragging behind him the misshapen prisoner. Beauroneaux appeared unfazed. "You do see, Bo – I can call you Bo, can't I? – that the boy's head looks like a bird cage. And he has three eyes."

"How do I know he wasn't born that way?" Beauroneaux said warily. Experience had taught him that these local municipalities were always making a mountain out of a molehill, looking for a government handout.

"He was fine the other day," Phigg said tersely, gritting his teeth, "and he took a bite out of my deputy here. Show him, Dorp." The deputy dutifully rolled up his sleeve and revealed his wound, which was now festering with an odorous plague.

"Sounds like an isolated incident," Beauroneaux said, and he started to rise out of his seat.

Phigg thought fast. "Ah yes, maybe you're right, Bo. But I tell you what," Phigg placated quickly, rising out of his chair and moving towards his liquor cabinet. He obscured the County Commissioner's view of the cabinet as he opened it, as the remnants of Enid Bountiface, who he had devoured after their tryst the previous afternoon, were stored inside. "Let's have a little drink, since you came all the way out here to our little burg on such a hot day." He brought the vase of moonshine over to the desk and poured some into a pencil-holder, offering it towards his guest.

Beauroneaux's long stint as a County Commissioner had also taught him that it was not wise to reject the hospitality of the bumpkin populace, no matter how crude or backwoods. Without much looking at his host or the beverage proffered, he shrugged his shoulders and drank it down. Phigg's rats' eyes narrowed as he waited for Beauroneaux's reaction. The pasty man grew an even whiter shade of pale, and looked for a moment as if he was about to vomit, but instead, let out a huge belch, only to discover that his tongue had swelled to the size of a grapefruit – it dangled out from between his lips, and sprouted an eye, which blinked back at Beauroneaux. "I think the disease may be spreading, though," the mayor said nonchalantly.

"I thee what you mean," Beauroneaux sighed.

"So… Now that you see the extent of the severity of the problem that we have on our hands down heah," Phigg said, leaning back in his chair with a satisfied air, "I was thinking that if you could see fit to get the big boys up at the capitol to release just a teensy bit of their rainy day funds, we could have us here a sort of public awareness and containment program put into place, in a manner of speaking."

"Yeth, that might be betht," the County Commissioner lisped, as his tongue wagged and its pupil rolled. He was now seeing triple, and in two directions.

"In fact," Phigg continued, "since there's no time to waste, if you could secure a commitment this afternoon, I think we could arrange to have a big ol' town meeting this very Sunday, up at the field of Slogg's Farm, and we can start gettin' this whole monster matter under control."

"I thee," Beauroneaux replied, and he tried to get out of his seat again, but found that his balance was wobbly.

"Need a hand?" the mayor asked, pulling one out of the liquor cabinet.

CHAPTER 20
CATECHISM OF THE CLOVEN GOSPEL

By the end of the week, the ministry of Reverend Horel Burnbroom was breathing new flames from its fire and brimstone pulpit. The congregation had swelled from two wayward chickens to enough semi-human beings to count on three hands, which many of the parishioners had. To accommodate this influx of attendants, bales of hay were arranged in a semi-circle around the egg-crate pulpit, from which the good Reverend was sermonizing with fervor.

"I had me a vision, good people. A vision so magnificent, so unearthly, so very pink and pudgy, so as to make our life here on this Earth seem but a faint fantasy by comparison." Burnbroom's monk-cut circle of hair flapped as he shook his head in wonder to underscore his words. "I saw the face of our savior, the face o' the future o' the human race – and how was that face? Round as the sun, smiling from its snout – friends, the man in the moon is not a man at all. The great God that circles above, that will unite us in our destiny, is not of human form."

"Oink!" shouted Burnbroom's flock, in unison.

"That's right, my friends." Burnbroom picked up a book from the altar – it was the Bible, now covered in pigskin, like a football for the great game of life. "It is not man that was created in God's image. It was the pig! And thusly, a hog shall lead us! A humongous hog in Heaven above!"

"Oink!" Again, the mutant worshippers echoed the

passions emanating from the pulpit.

"And a great rain has come down upon the land, and that rain has filled our tub of holy water to the brimful." At this cue, the Reverend's altar boy (so to speak), a goat named Baphazol, came in from the outside, hauling a lead bathtub with clawed feet behind him by means of a rope tied around his tail. Burnbroom dunked his hand into the tub, which was still half-full of the skull-toad sky-water from the storm several days before. He now walked among those sitting on bales of hay, dripping green drops of drizzle on the foreheads of the faithful. Sizzling sounds flew up from their flesh as their eyes crossed to receive this benediction from above.

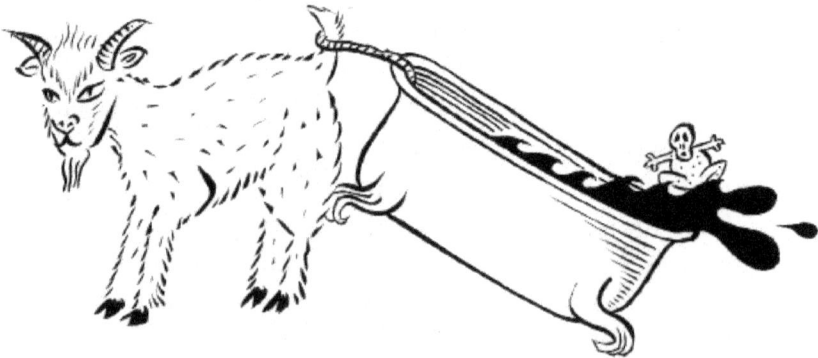

Having anointed all in attendance, the Reverend returned to his station, and stretched out his arms in proclamation. "And our band of believers is only the beginning! Soon the whole town will join us in our knowledge, as I foresee a Salvation Revival Meetin' and Gospel Healin', a-comin' this very Sunday, on the slopes of Slogg's Farm, just on the edge of town, where there's space enough to accommodate all the good people that will hear the truthful word!" Oinks erupted all around in excitement.

Unfortunately, this moment of religious rapture was interrupted by a loud popping sound, followed by a slurping noise. A buck-toothed, pig-tailed young woman in the middle of the floor had just bitten a chunk out of the torso of poor Pudweena Harff, who was sitting next to her on the bale of hay.

"Miss Floretta, please refrain from eating in church," Burnbroom admonished. The girl grinned back sheepishly, blood dripping down her blouse.

CHAPTER 21

THE LAST FAIR DEAL IN TOWN, GONE DOWN THRICE

Come Saturday, Mayor T. B. Phigg made his way by jalopy up to the Slogg Farm. He had Deputy Dorp come with him, primarily to unroll a long carpet on which he would walk so as to avoid the grubs and bloodworms that infested the ground. It proved additionally useful today, as Dorp had to unroll it all the way onto the muddy floor of the pigpen, which now sprouted a wooden sign upon which was scrawled "SLOGG'S HOG: 25 SENTS PER LOOK." Phigg looked upon the sign with curiosity, which was quickly satisfied when he saw the massive form of Slogg's Hog, who was sitting serenely in his own filth, and surrounded by a motley collection of gawkers, who seemed to be in some sort of stupor. Phigg spotted Farmer Slogg and had Dorp position the carpet in his direction.

"Herconium! I see you're now in the roadside attraction business," Phigg bellowed in greeting to Slogg head #1, who nodded back slowly. The last time Mayor Phigg had come onto the property, it was with the county health inspector, who had to be fed to the pigs with the help of Daisy's serrated steel. "I've come to see about rentin' out a corner of your property on the morrow for a little civic gathering I'm plannin'."

Slogg #1 opened his mouth, but the reply came from his twin brother on the left side. "Yew kin talk to me 'bout thet, guv'nor," drawled the second Slogg. "My brother ain't got much of a head fer bizness. It'll cost ya twenny-five dollars."

Phigg shifted his stance slightly so as to face the talking head. "That'll be fine," said Mayor Phigg, and with both hands, shook the paws of both brothers. He then sauntered back towards his motorcar, as Deputy Dorp followed behind him, rolling up the carpet beneath his feet. No sooner had the automobile departed in a cloud of exhaust fumes, than Slogg received another auspicious visitor. Walking up the path from the road was the good Reverend Burnbroom, with his flock of followers right behind him. Burnbroom was carrying a large wooden staff with what looked like strips of bacon tacked to it; a halo of flies buzzed about the macabre implement. Burnbroom and his gaggle were all dressed in robes made from feed-sacks.

Slogg #2 approached the Reverend in an attempt to collect his visitors' fees, but as soon as Burnbroom set eyes on Slogg's Hog, he burst into wild exhortations of a religious nature. "He lives! He breathes! The mountainous Mammal of the Mysteries, manifested! Harrooooharraaahoooo!" The Reverend brushed by the two-headed farmer and got on his knees before the big pig, along with the members of his ministry, joining the handful of folks that were already prostrate in the mud in front of the boar. The hog's third eye was open and rotating, and Burnbroom was instantly hypnotized into silence.

Slogg #2 was just about to drag his brother over to this newly-landed clutch of true believers in order to extract a toll charge, when Churlotta Lovelorn came over the pigpen fence. She addressed Slogg #1 cheerfully. "Well howdy-do, Herconium! Whatcha got goin' on here?"

"Oh howdy, Miss Churlotta. I've just been housin' my hog."

"And it'll cost ya twenty-five cents to see 'im," Slogg #2 chimed in greedily.

Churlotta fished a quarter from her sock and handed it over. "Well, I do just love me them pigs lately," she said, and wandered over by the rest. When she saw Slogg's Hog in all his three-eyed hugeness, she was moved in a way that none of those present were, and boldly went where none had; she strode right up to the two-thousand pound pink wonder and reached and put her hand on his fuzzy forehead, next to the third eye, and she softly sang:

"Put yer hand in the ham and get back to the land
Ever'body praise the pork and spare the spork"

When she was finished, she sauntered back to Farmer Slogg, and addressing his original head, said, "I'd like ta have a music show here tomorrow."

"Why shore, Churlotta, that'd be swell."

"It'll cost ya twenny five doll hairs," Slogg #2 interjected.

Churlotta ignored the greedy twin. "Thanks, Herconium, I'll see y'all tomorrow," she said and bounced on down the road, humming to herself.

Soon after, Burnbroom woke from his trance and came back from his audience with the hypnotic hog, his cult members in close concert behind him. He approached the brothers Slogg. "My dear keepers of the Heavenly Hog, I propose that we hold a mass on this very Sunday, and that…"

Slogg #2 interrupted him, holding out his left hand. "Twenny-five dollers."

Burnbroom turned to his dozen followers in their feed-sack vestments. "Pay the men," he instructed.

CHAPTER 22
THE NEWS HE BRINGS TO CREEPING THINGS

By midnight on Saturday, calm had returned to the pigpen. Farmer Slogg was asleep in the outhouse, his two heads snoring soundly against the toilet seat. The gaggle of gawkers had dispersed for the night, all eagerly anticipating the following day's big concert-rally-revival. All was not quite quiet in the muddy pigpen, however... Under the light of a full yellow moon, a slew of critters had come to join Slogg's Hog. Some had slithered through the weeds, and others had fluttered through the trees. Owls, bluebirds, and buzzards rested their wings on the fence posts, while weasels and opossums crouched in the dirt, along with the grubs and bloodworms that had made their way in from the fields. Lizards and ocelots had crept down from the hills and goats and sheep, gone AWOL from neighboring farms, mingled among them. Housecats and dogs had snuck away from their masters' hearths as well, instinctively drawn to Slogg's Hog, for what purpose they did not yet know. One Siamese kitten balanced a fishbowl on her nose so that a goldfish could join the assemblage. The ducks and geese from far-flung ponds ruffled their feathers. They had all instinctively answered the great boar's telepathic call, and now they sat around him at midnight, predator and prey alike, chirping and purring softly. They sensed that this mammoth mammal was their master, and they gathered below his great girth and warm, crud-encrusted skin with its fine pink hairs. Then, in a language of oinks and honks indecipherable to man but plain to all other species, he spoke.

"Creatures of the wood, of the wind, of the earth and of the seas and sand... Our time is nearly at hand. I have drunk of the mystic toad rain, and the space-frogs have given me dominion over our wayward human cousins. On the morrow, I shall at last bring them into our fold. Spread the word, fish and fowl and beast and bug, to your flocks and herds!" The collection of critters erupted into a cacophony of hoots and bleats of excitement.

CHAPTER 23
HAMERICA

Come midnight at the office of the mayor, T.B. Phigg and his deputy were hard at work, which was nearly as strange an occurrence as what was happening across town at Slogg's Farm. "Put some more exclamation points on that!" T.B. instructed Deputy Dorp, who was, to the best of his ability, lettering a handbill as the mayor dictated to him. So far, it read: "ATTENSON SITISENS OF SLOGG HOLLER!!! EMERJENSY TOWN MEETIN UP AT SLOGG FARM THIS SUNDAY TODAY TO ADRESS MONSTER…"

The two public servants contemplated how to continue the sentence. "Problem?" Dorp suggested hopefully.

"No, most of the folks 'round here already got a touch o' this monster thing, myself included." He stroked his nether region gingerly. "They may be monsterized, but they's still voters. I don't wanna alienate my constituency… Just say 'issue.'"

Dorp painstakingly wrote the word down, and then read it back. "…TO ADDRESS MONSTER IS YOU. What's that mean, T.B.?"

"Oh, never mind, just say 'to address monsters,' which is what I'm gonna be doin'." Phigg took a sip from the vase of toad-shine and got a faraway look in his beady little eyes. "I tell ya Dorp, I see great things ahead. I see me at the state capitol, but instead of flyin' flags we is fryin' bacon, and that big pig is beside me, with a whole chamber of mutant flunkies, and a cabinet o' curiosities in the house o' pigs…"

"Want me to run these off on the copier, T.B.?"

"Yep, and then I want you to deliver 'em all to every doorstep in town, so that the peoples is thoroughly notified."

"But that'll take forever, T.B.," Dorp whined.

"Take the Cragmire kid with you."

"But… he's a cannibal!"

"Now, Dorp, we gone have to get with the times. We's all cannibals now, or soon will be, I predict. There's no stoppin' progress."

Dorp mused on this for a moment. "But he ate my arm!"

"Here, have some o' this frog-water, it's a powerful growth aid," the mayor said to his deputy, handing over the vase of tainted moonshine from the Charlip still. Dorp drank a mouthful, and indeed, soon had a new appendage to replace his damaged one.

CHAPTER 24
FOULER AND FOWL-ER

The witching hour also found Reverend Burnbroom in a frenzy of activity. He and his confused cult were gathered at the back of Burnbroom's barn, amassing a pile of tires that they had purloined from motorcars parked on Mane Street. "Smelt them with Holy Fire," Burnbroom shrieked, and one of his congregants dutifully doused them with lighter fluid and threw on a match. The circle of true believers gathered around the flaming rubber bonfire that erupted, breathing in the noxious fumes of Firestones on fire.

Burnbroom stripped off his cardboard clerical collar and feed sack vestments, his exposed scarred skin glowing pasty white by the fetid fireside. "Now roll them on my back, my faithful!" he instructed, throwing himself on the ground. None of the dozen church-members moved. "Take the wheels of fire, and roll over my bones!" he yelled, more forcefully. His followers then endeavored to remove the tires from the pyre by manipulating wooden planks pulled from the walls of the church-barn. They maneuvered the smoldering rubber wheels over to the prostrate Reverend, pushing the melting rubber circles over his back as Burnbroom writhed in the most exquisite pain he'd yet experienced.

Self-torture was not his primary ambition on this moonlit night, however. The rolling of the burning tires over his back had left a sticky slick of black tar on his skin. "Now pluck them chickens!" he gasped. Though most of the chickens in town had fled to the side of the big pig, two of the dumber hens were still flapping about the churchyard this evening, and had the misfortune of being captured by Burnbroom's sack-robed minions. As they held the hapless birds, Burnbroom further instructed, "But don't hurt 'em. They is our brethren. We will be like the chicken, to be closer to the pig." The chickens replied that there was no way that plucking their feathers would not hurt them, but it just sounded like squawking to the religious fanatics, who soon had shorn the chickens of their feathers. "Now stick 'em on me," Burnbroom ordered, and his minions shoved the feathers into the Reverend's flesh, where they remained, stuck securely to the tire tar. When it was done, Reverend Horel Burnbroom fully resembled the birdbrain that he was.

"Now y'all do the same," he decreed, and his servants solemnly shed their sacks to follow in their feathered fellow's footsteps.

CHAPTER 25
HOW THE TWANG WAS TWUNG

Churlotta Lovelorn and Her Hollerin' Frogbottoms had been rehearsing since the sun went down, or rather had tried to, or to be even more accurate, Fuzz and Dormutt were engaged in a four hour progressive math rock experimental jam that created such a furious cacophony that Churlotta was unable to fit in a strum edge-wise. Her sixteen-limbed rhythm section was completely lost in their spasmodic instrumental noodling. She had to climb up on the hollow log that formed Dormutt's bass guitar and rap him on the head to get his attention.

"Whut?" he asked, his seventeen fingers still twiddling furiously.

"It's midnight, boys, we need to start practicing for the big concert tomorrow."

"We are practicing," Dormutt replied, slapping the log-bass's cat-intestine strings to produce a funky resonation as Fuzz executed a thirty-second note paradiddle (an extremely difficult percussion flourish) with three arms waving five chopsticks.

"Um, well, don't you think you're…" Churlotta searched for the most tactful word. "Overplayin'. Just a tad."

Dormutt regarded her with a withering expression through half-closed eyelids. "Don't impede our musical progress," he said.

"Yeah, don't empty our music o' frogs legs," Fuzz echoed imperfectly.

Churlotta turned an angry shade of red, and swiftly snapped one of Dormutt's two catgut bass strings and then broke three of Fuzz's six chopsticks. Her point made, and her rhythm sections now forced into a simpler accompaniment, Churlotta joined in and sang her song:

"I been down in the dirt too long
But a heavenly rain done finally come
All my thoughts is thunk and all my drinks been drunk
On my grave just put a puddle
So the fishes can come wiggle"

CHAPTER 26
SUFFERIN' SIBLINGS

Sunday morning was coming down over Slogg's Holler with a fluorescent orange sky in tow, augmented by purple swirls of pregnant clouds glimmering above, wielding the promise of more weird weather. From where they were perched atop the slope in front of their outhouse, the Slogg Farmers stood on their single pair of legs, eyeing the gathering storm. "Looks like the Devil's gettin' married today," both heads muttered, squinting at where the day-glo sun met the menacing rainclouds.

The second Slogg craned his head down in the opposite direction, stretching the delicate tendons between them, to survey the scene below on the farm. "Looks like lots o' customers comin' in," he said. Indeed, a stream of folks were heading into Slogg's Farm, stumbling up in three large groups. First came Deputy Dorp and the mutant, elbow-biting Cragmire kid, marching forward and carrying signs that displayed the same vague message as the handbills they'd printed the previous night. Mayor T. B. Phigg followed slowly behind them in his motorcar, and behind him, shambling on an excess of limbs, were the former cream of Slogg's Holler society: the bankers and bakers, sewing ladies and other cornerstones of the community, grown even weirder with the effects of the polluted pork products. They had left their homes on Mane Street to fall in line behind their elected officials.

To their left, the mystic flock of Reverend Burnbroom,

now tarred and feathered, flapped their arms and clucked like chickens as they fluttered forward, followed by dozens of the town's more derelict denizens – fringe folk formerly shut up in attics, along with plenty of the impressionable elderly, now drafted into Burnbroom's fold.

A third group pulled up the rear, a noisy bunch of rabble; they were the farm hands, cheating wives and common creeps of Slogg's Holler. They drank and caroused in the wake of a flatbed truck, on top of which Churlotta Lovelorn and her Hollerin' Frogbottoms were performing. A few line-danced with their many legs as the parade weaved towards Slogg's Farm, while Churlotta sang:

"Come n' gather round the meaty mountain
Drink y'all from the toad-rain fountain
I saw a flyin' sausage in the sky"

As the three tributaries of half-human traffic converged at the entrance to Slogg's Farm's fallow fields, the purple clouds grew darker and a soft sprinkle began. As before, it was a drizzle of skull-headed amphibious frogs that began to fall down towards the ground. Farmer Slogg #1 caught one directly in his mouth and chewed thoughtfully.

Farmer Slogg the second, looking down upon the approaching masses, attempted to rub his hands together greedily, but having only one hand willing, he instead whistled greedily and said, "Now we gone make a fortune."

"How so?" inquired Farmer Slogg #1.

"Well we is gone charge all o' them, o' course!"

"No we ain't," the original Slogg stated firmly.

"This'n our land, dangit. Don't you be tryin' my patience now."

"I'm sick o' yer schemin' ways," Herconium Siliam Slogg retorted, raising his one right fist towards the ugly mutant head that sprouted from the left side of his neck. Slogg #2 laughed, his black teeth wobbling in the morning breeze.

"Whut you gonna do, brother? We is two halves o' one hole."

The original Farmer Slogg gulped loudly, swallowing the rest of the death's head frog. He spat out the skull, which landed in the other Slogg's eye cavity. "I'm hungry," Slogg #1 said, and with a strange stretching sound, he opened his mouth supernaturally wide and with a great gnashing of his several teeth, bit off his brother's head.

As a rivulet of dark arterial blood spewed upwards from the right side of his neck, the detached noggin of his former twin sat momentarily within the engorged mouth of Farmer Slogg. He contemplated chewing on it, but in the end spat it out so that it would no longer be a part of him.

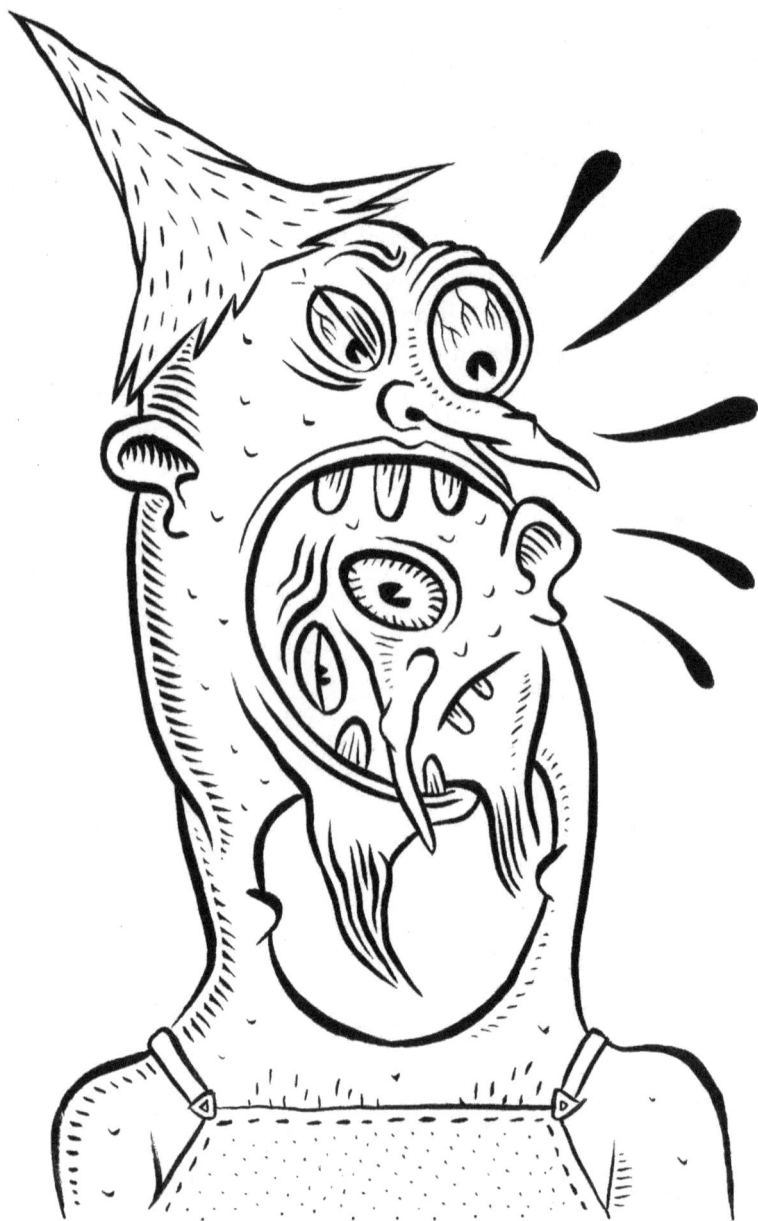

CHAPTER 27
THE DEGENERATE ELECTORATE

The three factions of Slogg's Holler made their way onto the worm-infested ground of Farmer Slogg's farm for the big concert-rally-revival, following either Reverend Burnbroom, Mayor Phigg or Churlotta and her band. As they became aware of the strange rain sprinkling down again, many laid down in the mud and opened up their mouths to catch the critters dropping from above. Some of the skull-headed frogs landed directly in the ever-bubbling vat of frying oil in the corner of the pen. The once-again single-minded Farmer Slogg gathered these crispy critters into his pocket when they turned golden brown, and hobbling about on his hoof, he distributed them to the assembled townsfolk, who gobbled them down ravenously. The already-twisted crowd grew rapidly more mutated as they ingested this additional bounty of the mysterious delicacies. In addition, there was the fierce appetite that eating the sky-toads instilled as biting one of the weird creatures only resulted in greater hunger. They began to turn on one another, neighbor eating neighbor in a gross display of cannibal fever.

Mayor Tiligree Beronius Phigg erroneously judged this as a moment worth seizing. He jumped into the pigpen and positioned himself in front of Slogg's Hog, who eyed him warily. Then Mayor Phigg called to Deputy Dorp. "Git on yer knees," he said, which the deputy dutifully did. Phigg then stood on Dorp's back and addressed the crowd.

"Folks, I see that y'all are hungry. Well, lemme give you

95

this to chew on. We know that the pig…" he drew out the syllable, waving his small rodentious arms towards the mighty hog behind him, "…has the power. These be strange times upon us. But these is our times, my fellow Slogg Hollerians! We have been ignored until now. The big men may say we're just a bunch o' bumpkins. They may say we is monsters! Well, that may be so…" There were a few nods of approval from the rambunctious crowd, some of them pausing in mid-bite upon their neighbors' noses.

"But the weather itself is on our side!" Phigg pointed to the purple clouds and their odd, amphibious drizzle. "And now we shall sail forth on this glorious tide of scaly critters come down from the sky. We are gonna demand our right to grow as many arms and knees as we please!" He swept his arm back towards Slogg's Hog, who rolled his three eyes. "And as right hand to the ham… I will lead us!"

Phigg stood silent with his arms outstretched, and his audience, who had momentarily paused in their rabid ingestion of the sky-frogs and each other, was unsure how to react. Suddenly, Slogg's Hog riled up his massive pink belly and bellowed forth a momentous, deafening "OINK!" that knocked Phigg right off his bent deputy and into the mud of the pen, where he sank deeply.

CHAPTER 28
THE PORK PULPIT

Watching the mayor's failure of a speech gave Reverend Burnbroom time to compose himself, and with the politician lying still in the mud, Burnbroom was able to take the damp, filthy floor for himself. He strode into the pigpen and waved his feathered arms in the air, sermonizing at the top of his lungs.

"Faithful friends, we all have sinned before the spirit of the slovenly swine! We all have been ignorant. Been ignorant of the gospels of Saint Francis – lover of the fanged and feathered, be they great or slimy. The age of man be at an end!" He swung his tarred arms, fluttering about like an angry pigeon as he preached to the perverted. "We wear this glorious plumage 'cuz we is one with the critters that swoop, swim and slither! The glorious kingdom to come, my friends, is the Animal Kingdom!"

Burnbroom's already feverish mind was cranking and clanking away madly, and he stumbled on an idea – a plan of action that would cement his righteousness in the annals of the devout. A way he could take his place alongside the greatest prophets of history and stand tall as a man of the cloth in the hall of martyrs up in Heaven.

"The canine jaws of Mother Earth are barking at us!" He screamed, turning bright red as he leapt up and down before the bemused cannibals clustered alongside the pigpen fence. "Her savage seed is sown by torrents of death and scales from the skies! The answer is clear!"

His audience, as mutated and bloodthirsty as they had become, still retained a sliver of their faculties for logical reasoning, and accordingly, struggled to discern what Burnbroom was getting at. They looked at him quizzically, and he knew it was time to act.

"The tables and tide have done turned! The hunter is now the hunted, as God above has decreed that the Beast shall regain its dominion o'er the land! We must sacrifice ourselves to the slaughter!" And then, with a great leap of faith, Reverend Horel Burnbroom ran towards Slogg's Hog and with his feathered ams forced himself into the mighty mammal's big pink mouth.

He hoped to be chewed and swallowed, and thus immortalized as the first son of man to be swallowed by the heavenly ham.

There was an awkward moment as Burnbroom waited with eyes closed inside the jaws of Slogg's Hogg, anticipating his deliverance into the afterlife. The crowd of cretins stood silent as the big pig sniffed Burnbroom curiously with his stupendous snout, and then unceremoniously spat him out.

CHAPTER 29
HOEDOWN OF HORRORS

Meanwhile, Churlotta Lovelorn and her Hollerin' Frogbottoms were struggling to get their frying pan and hollow log in tune; the bumpy ride in the flatbed truck had left them more dissonant than usual. Dormutt was stretching out the cat intestines that served as his bass strings, and Churlotta banged her banjo against one of the fence posts until they judged their instruments to be within a country mile of each other, tonally speaking. They then stepped gingerly over the bodies of Mayor Phigg and Reverend Burnbroom, positioning themselves in the center of the muddy pigpen. The townsfolk gathered around them, excitement building as the orange sky above reached its peak of illumination. The crimson clouds continued to rain down boneheaded amphibians as well, which made the already sloppy confines of Slogg's Farm's pigpen even slimier. Churlotta's two band mates and her rambunctious mutant audience were gulping down this green rain of hybrid creatures with open mouths, and Churlotta figured she'd better launch into a song before things got even more out of hand.

She looked behind her to Fuzz and Dormutt as she counted to four, and saw Slogg's Hog wink at her with his third eye as he loomed over them all. She plucked her frying-pan banjo and began:

"There's a hog up in heaven who's a hunnerd miles wide
And you won't eat his bacon 'cuz his skin is full of eyes

I been down in the dirt too long
But a heavenly rain done finally come
All my thoughts is thunk and all my drinks been drunk
Now I roll in the mud and stink like a skunk

Keep my beat with pigs' feet
An' bleat with shaggy sheep
On my grave just put a puddle
So the fishes can come wiggle

The pink belly bounces
A spiral eye pronounces
Where the fields are fallow we shall follow
We will grovel, we will wallow
Like a big pig's behind
Life is a pork rind

Come n' gather round the meaty mountain
Drink y'all from the toad-rain fountain
I saw a flyin' sausage in the sky
Put yer hand in the ham and get back to the land
Ever'body praise the pork and spare the spork"

At this point the Hollerin' Frogbottoms launched into an instrumental passage, and Churlotta noticed that the crowd was getting rowdier in ever more peculiar ways. As the new wave of skull-headed frogs worked their wily metamorphoses on the peoples' physiology, new limbs sprouted from odd locations with sickly popping noises. The audience's swaying bodies were distending and distorting in various directions as the yokels continued to dance to the Frogbottoms' hootenanny sound, lurching and throbbing like parasites in the bloodstream. They shrieked and moaned as the fierce appetites instilled in them by the mutant toads led to debauched acts both carnal and culinary in nature. Most had shed their clothes in the mud, and their panoply of fleshy humps and hollows were rubbing against one another in abandon – what body parts were not being eaten were being inserted as a sensuous orgy of orifices oscillated into a hedonistic excess of mutant monster cannibal lovemaking.

Daughter of the Lost Cause Pudweena Harff had removed her dentures from the original of her three mouths, and with a great sucking sound had swallowed the birdcage-shaped head of the Cragmire boy. Also doing her part to close the generation gap, nonagenarian Grimelda Futzwig was leaning against a fencepost with her six legs wrapped around young Elwore Furbich as she licked his earlobe with one mouth and bit off his nose with her other. Elwore's sister Horphense rubbed her three breasts against the stunned figure of Deputy Dorp, who took a bite out of each. Not to be outdone, the slatternly Floretta was engaged in a shameful display of arousal with the curl of Wallace Wallbog's well-oiled lock of hair, at the same time as she has digesting his nether regions. Within moments, they were two bloody stumps rolling in a slick of brown goo. Back on the floor of the pigpen, and with all political aspirations put aside, T. B. Phigg was engaged in a morbid fit of self-stimulation. He tugged with one hand on his trouser snake while biting off the fingers on his other, moaning ecstatically all the while.

Churlotta continued to strum her banjo as she gaped in wonder at the hideous weirdness erupting around her. "Maybe mama was right 'bout the sinful influence of pop'lar music," she thought. Eventually she came to realize that her backing band was sounding strange – the bass had dropped out and only an erratic backbeat remained. She turned around to see that Fuzz was banging his spittoon snare drum with Dormutt's arm, and the rest of Dormutt was nowhere to be seen, except for a few toes sticking out of one of Fuzz's drooling mouths, and Fuzz's belly was swollen to a ghastly degree. Then little old Pudweena Harff rocketed up from the mud to attack Fuzz with her dentures, biting a hole in his neck that led him to deflate like a child's balloon. His last shreds of skin flapped in the breeze and then drifted away.

"Reckon I've gone solo now," Churlotta mused.

CHAPTER 30
PINK PERSUASION

And then, the two thousand pound pig emitted a stupendous snort – a snort from its snout that sounded with a volume that reverberated through the fields and echoed off the neighboring hills. This snort made the muddy ground ripple and the trees bend as all the skull-headed frogs still on the ground or coming down from the sky were inhaled into the great mouth of Slogg's Hog with a massive sucking sound. After slurping up the last bone-toad into his mountainous, fine-haired belly, the massive mammal began to slowly levitate up from the muddy floor of the pigpen.

All the monstrous townsfolk stopped their cavorting and stared at the big pink pig, which was now hovering above the assembled throng. He opened his third eye, and it began to rotate. The retina became a purple spiral, and as it turned it emanated a mesmeric influence that entranced the slack-jawed yokels below… Silence reigned, except for an ethereal hum vibrating forth from the great floating beast fifty feet above.

Farmer Slogg felt his shriveled old brain enraptured as he gazed at his huge, levitating farm animal. He felt suddenly infused with an earthy energy, and instinctively dove down to the muddy floor of the pigpen and rolled around, his naked body turning brown as he flopped and slopped about. Old Missus Futzwig, who a moment before had been simultaneously molesting and ingesting poor Elwore Furbich, dropped the body part she was sucking on and also fell into the mud, rolling back and forth and kicking her legs in the air joyously. Reverend Burnbroom, who was gazing up at the pig's powerful pupil along with the rest, found a sudden release from his mortal aspirations and shrieked with glee, writhing in the dirt like a worm.

Slogg's Hog continued to beam down his mysterious mesmeric influence like a dirigible releasing a toxic gas, and soon a critical mass was reached. The power of the Hypno-Hog

influenced the crowd of cretins' craniums towards a peaceful primitiveness – a simplified state of satisfaction. With a
massive splashing sound, all the mutated men and women of
Slogg's Holler dropped to the floor of the pigpen, or into the
fallow fields of Slogg's Farm (which were now damp from the
recent rain of slimy sky-toads). They wriggled and wallowed
in the dirty earth. Devoid of clothing they moaned in ecstasy,
but they were no longer attacking each other – all were now
content to roll about in the grime, squealing like pigs, totally
enthralled with the sensual sensation of the cool mud on their
skin beneath the hot mid-day sun. Churlotta, though a little
less frenzied than the rest, also felt this earthy inclination; she
shed her dress, got down on the land, and dug in with her
hands. "Oink," she softly sang.

CHAPTER 31
THE DIVINE FILTH

As mid-day slid towards afternoon, the monstrous mutants of Slogg's Holler were still playing in the mud beneath a floating pig. Churlotta sat up on her elbows and surveyed the scene... All around her, the townspeople that she had known all her life no longer resembled people at all. With the biological changes that the toad-rain and its infection via fried pork had brought, they now resembled some kind of land crab, with their multiple limbs and swollen mounds of skin. Free of clothing, they had continued to wallow in the wet ground en masse for hours now. Neighbors that had been at each other's throats frolicked as if in a kiddy pool, covering each other in mud and hog slop.

"Least it's peaceful," Churlotta sighed, thinking back on the chaos of the past few days, and she looked up at Slogg's Hog, who was smiling widely as he hovered in the sky, sending down his mesmeric influence. Then his two non-hypnotic eyes turned towards Churlotta, and Slogg's Hog spoke to her in a voice that only she could hear.

"Good show, Churlotta," he said with perfect pig-diction.

"I guess so..." she replied. "Everyone seems happy."

"Oh yes," Slogg's Hog agreed, nodding his massive pink orb of a head.

"They don't seem to be tryin' to eat each other no more. And they's not so concerned with humpin' each other, neither," Churlotta continued. "They seem just pleased as punch to be wrigglin' in the mud like animals." Churlotta looked around her and marveled at her fellow man, now reveling in the simple joys of being sub-human. "I mean, people around here always kinda acted like animals, but not so much in a good way," she said to the great pig in the sky.

Slogg's Hog winked once more at Churlotta, and then his hypnotic third eye ceased to be a spiral. His mesmeric emanations had ceased, but the good semi-people of Slogg's Holler continued to frolic in the mud, behaving like pigs. The big boar slowly floated back down to the earth and joined them all in the mud, rolling slowly about in his pigpen. Churlotta closed her eyes and smiled. The damp mud felt good on her skin, cool and somehow clean in its filthiness. She heard the chirping of birds and the mooing of calves as the animals came in from the surrounding meadows, basking alongside the mutant townsfolk beneath the summer sun. Soon the snakes slithered down from the mountains and the squirrels crept down from the trees; all manner of creature came to join in the massive mud bath.

As the day grew long and edged towards dusk, Farmer Slogg stuck his head out of the dirt long enough to look around at the party raging on in his pasture. The opossums that had once invaded his family home were now sitting next to him, and he smiled with all his six teeth at the serene scene. As the sun set slowly over Slogg's Holler, it seemed unlikely that any of its citizens would ever do much of anything else again, other than wallow in the mud, slurping up slop, and that was good.

Bizarro books

CATALOG   SPRING 2011

Bizarro Books publishes under the following imprints:

www.rawdogscreamingpress.com

www.eraserheadpress.com

www.afterbirthbooks.com

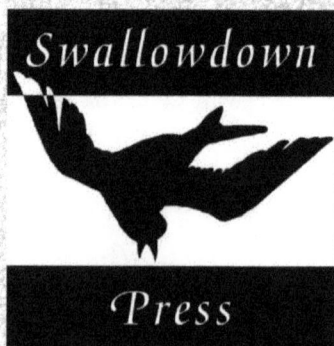

www.swallowdownpress.com

For all your Bizarro needs visit:

WWW.BIZARROCENTRAL.COM

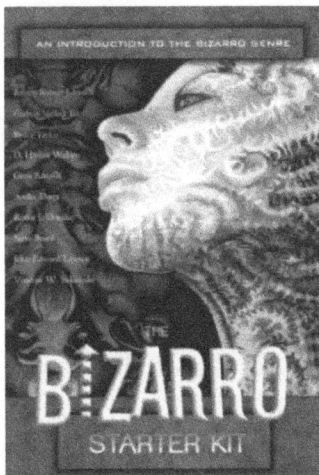

Introduce yourselves to the bizarro fiction genre and all of its authors with the Bizarro Starter Kit series. Each volume features short novels and short stories by ten of the leading bizarro authors, designed to give you a perfect sampling of the genre for only $10.

BB-0X1
"The Bizarro Starter Kit" (Orange)

Featuring D. Harlan Wilson, Carlton Mellick III, Jeremy Robert Johnson, Kevin L Donihe, Gina Ranalli, Andre Duza, Vincent W. Sakowski, Steve Beard, John Edward Lawson, and Bruce Taylor.
236 pages $10

BB-0X2
"The Bizarro Starter Kit" (Blue)

Featuring Ray Fracalossy, Jeremy C. Shipp, Jordan Krall, Mykle Hansen, Andersen Prunty, Eckhard Gerdes, Bradley Sands, Steve Aylett, Christian TeBordo, and Tony Rauch. **244 pages $10**

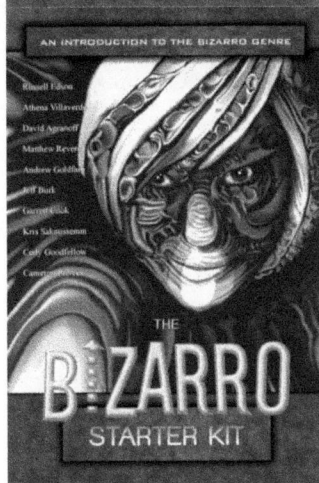

BB-0X2
"The Bizarro Starter Kit" (Purple)

Featuring Russell Edson, Athena Villaverde, David Agranoff, Matthew Revert, Andrew Goldfarb, Jeff Burk, Garrett Cook, Kris Saknussemm, Cody Goodfellow, and Cameron Pierce **264 pages $10**

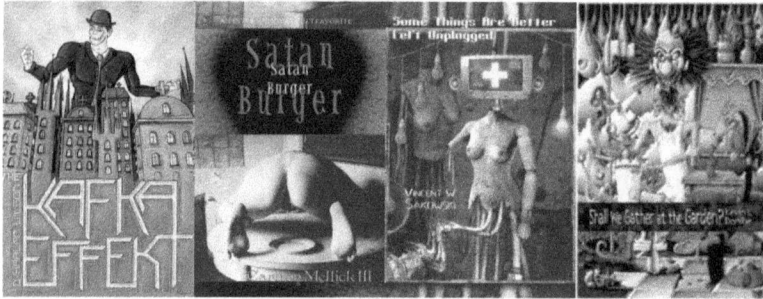

BB-001"The Kafka Effekt" D. Harlan Wilson - A collection of forty-four irreal short stories loosely written in the vein of Franz Kafka, with more than a pinch of William S. Burroughs sprinkled on top. **211 pages $14**

BB-002 "Satan Burger" Carlton Mellick III - The cult novel that put Carlton Mellick III on the map ... Six punks get jobs at a fast food restaurant owned by the devil in a city violently overpopulated by surreal alien cultures. **236 pages $14**

BB-003 "Some Things Are Better Left Unplugged" Vincent Sakwoski - Join The Man and his Nemesis, the obese tabby, for a nightmare roller coaster ride into this postmodern fantasy. **152 pages $10**

BB-004 "Shall We Gather At the Garden?" Kevin L Donihe - Donihe's Debut novel. Midgets take over the world, The Church of Lionel Richie vs. The Church of the Byrds, plant porn and more! **244 pages $14**

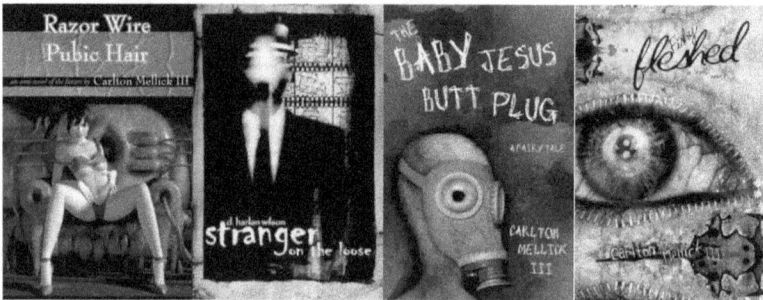

BB-005 "Razor Wire Pubic Hair" Carlton Mellick III - A genderless humandildo is purchased by a razor dominatrix and brought into her nightmarish world of bizarre sex and mutilation. **176 pages $11**

BB-006 "Stranger on the Loose" D. Harlan Wilson - The fiction of Wilson's 2nd collection is planted in the soil of normalcy, but what grows out of that soil is a dark, witty, otherworldly jungle... **228 pages $14**

BB-007 "The Baby Jesus Butt Plug" Carlton Mellick III - Using clones of the Baby Jesus for anal sex will be the hip sex fetish of the future. **92 pages $10**

BB-008 "Fishyfleshed" Carlton Mellick III - The world of the past is an illogical flatland lacking in dimension and color, a sick-scape of crispy squid people wandering the desert for no apparent reason. **260 pages $14**

BB-009 "Dead Bitch Army" Andre Duza - Step into a world filled with racist teenagers, cannibals, 100 warped Uncle Sams, automobiles with razor-sharp teeth, living graffiti, and a pissed-off zombie bitch out for revenge. **344 pages $16**

BB-010 "The Menstruating Mall" Carlton Mellick III - "The Breakfast Club meets Chopping Mall as directed by David Lynch." - Brian Keene **212 pages $12**

BB-011 "Angel Dust Apocalypse" Jeremy Robert Johnson - Meth-heads, man-made monsters, and murderous Neo-Nazis. "Seriously amazing short stories..." - Chuck Palahniuk, author of Fight Club **184 pages $11**

BB-012 "Ocean of Lard" Kevin L Donihe / Carlton Mellick III - A parody of those old Choose Your Own Adventure kid's books about some very odd pirates sailing on a sea made of animal fat. **176 pages $12**

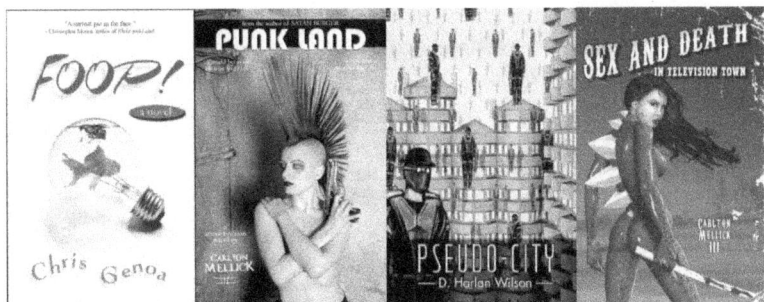

BB-015 "Foop!" Chris Genoa - Strange happenings are going on at Dactyl, Inc, the world's first and only time travel tourism company.
"A surreal pie in the face!" - Christopher Moore **300 pages $14**

BB-020 "Punk Land" Carlton Mellick III - In the punk version of Heaven, the anarchist utopia is threatened by corporate fascism and only Goblin, Mortician's sperm, and a blue-mohawked female assassin named Shark Girl can stop them. **284 pages $15**

BB-021"Pseudo-City" D. Harlan Wilson - Pseudo-City exposes what waits in the bathroom stall, under the manhole cover and in the corporate boardroom, all in a way that can only be described as mind-bogglingly irreal. **220 pages $16**

BB-023 "Sex and Death In Television Town" Carlton Mellick III - In the old west, a gang of hermaphrodite gunslingers take refuge from a demon plague in Telos: a town where its citizens have televisions instead of heads. **184 pages $12**

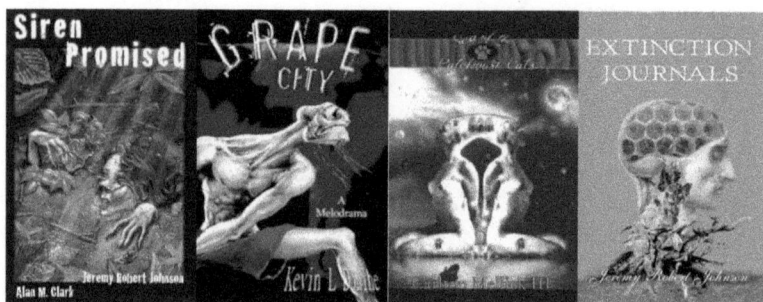

BB-027 "Siren Promised" Jeremy Robert Johnson & Alan M Clark
- Nominated for the Bram Stoker Award. A potent mix of bad drugs, bad dreams, brutal bad guys, and surreal/incredible art by Alan M. Clark. **190 pages $13**

BB-030 "Grape City" Kevin L. Donihe - More Donihe-style comedic bizarro about a demon named Charles who is forced to work a minimum wage job on Earth after Hell goes out of business. **108 pages $10**

BB-031"Sea of the Patchwork Cats" Carlton Mellick III - A quiet dreamlike tale set in the ashes of the human race. For Mellick enthusiasts who also adore The Twilight Zone. **112 pages $10**

BB-032 "Extinction Journals" Jeremy Robert Johnson - An uncanny voyage across a newly nuclear America where one man must confront the problems associated with loneliness, insane dieties, radiation, love, and an ever-evolving cockroach suit with a mind of its own. **104 pages $10**

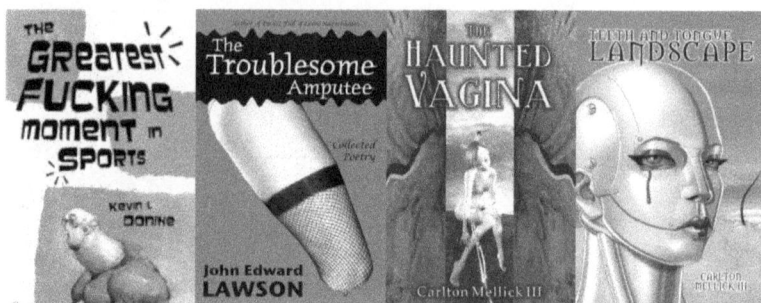

BB-034 "The Greatest Fucking Moment in Sports" Kevin L. Donihe
- In the tradition of the surreal anti-sitcom Get A Life comes a tale of triumph and agape love from the master of comedic bizarro. **108 pages $10**

BB-035 "The Troublesome Amputee" John Edward Lawson - Disturbing verse from a man who truly believes nothing is sacred and intends to prove it. **104 pages $9**

BB-037 "The Haunted Vagina" Carlton Mellick III - It's difficult to love a woman whose vagina is a gateway to the world of the dead. **132 pages $10**

BB-042 "Teeth and Tongue Landscape" Carlton Mellick III - On a planet made out of meat, a socially-obsessive monophobic man tries to find his place amongst the strange creatures and communities that he comes across. **110 pages $10**

BB-043 "War Slut" Carlton Mellick III - Part "1984," part "Waiting for Godot," and part action horror video game adaptation of John Carpenter's "The Thing." **116 pages $10**

BB-045 "Dr. Identity" D. Harlan Wilson - Follow the Dystopian Duo on a killing spree of epic proportions through the irreal postcapitalist city of Bliptown where time ticks sideways, artificial Bug-Eyed Monsters punish citizens for consumer-capitalist lethargy, and ultraviolence is as essential as a daily multivitamin. **208 pages $15**

BB-047 "Sausagey Santa" Carlton Mellick III - A bizarro Christmas tale featuring Santa as a piratey mutant with a body made of sausages. 124 pages $10

BB-048 "Misadventures in a Thumbnail Universe" Vincent Sakowski - Dive deep into the surreal and satirical realms of neo-classical Blender Fiction, filled with television shoes and flesh-filled skies. **120 pages $10**

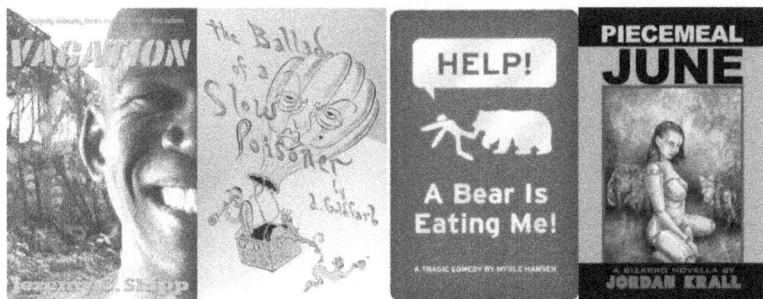

BB-049 "Vacation" Jeremy C. Shipp - Blueblood Bernard Johnson leaved his boring life behind to go on The Vacation, a year-long corporate sponsored odyssey. But instead of seeing the world, Bernard is captured by terrorists, becomes a key figure in secret drug wars, and, worse, doesn't once miss his secure American Dream. **160 pages $14**

BB-053 "Ballad of a Slow Poisoner" Andrew Goldfarb Millford Mutterwurst sat down on a Tuesday to take his afternoon tea, and made the unpleasant discovery that his elbows were becoming flatter. **128 pages $10**

BB-055 "Help! A Bear is Eating Me" Mykle Hansen - The bizarro, heartwarming, magical tale of poor planning, hubris and severe blood loss...
150 pages $11

BB-056 "Piecemeal June" Jordan Krall - A man falls in love with a living sex doll, but with love comes danger when her creator comes after her with crab-squid assassins. **90 pages $9**

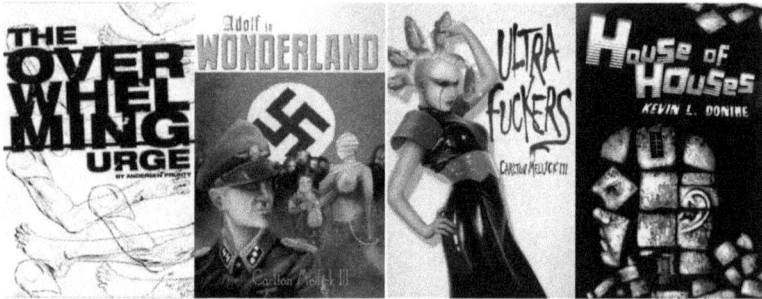

BB-058 "The Overwhelming Urge" Andersen Prunty - A collection of bizarro tales by Andersen Prunty. **150 pages $11**

BB-059 "Adolf in Wonderland" Carlton Mellick III - A dreamlike adventure that takes a young descendant of Adolf Hitler's design and sends him down the rabbit hole into a world of imperfection and disorder. **180 pages $11**

BB-061 "Ultra Fuckers" Carlton Mellick III - Absurdist suburban horror about a couple who enter an upper middle class gated community but can't find their way out. **108 pages $9**

BB-062 "House of Houses" Kevin L. Donihe - An odd man wants to marry his house. Unfortunately, all of the houses in the world collapse at the same time in the Great House Holocaust. Now he must travel to House Heaven to find his departed fiancee. **172 pages $11**

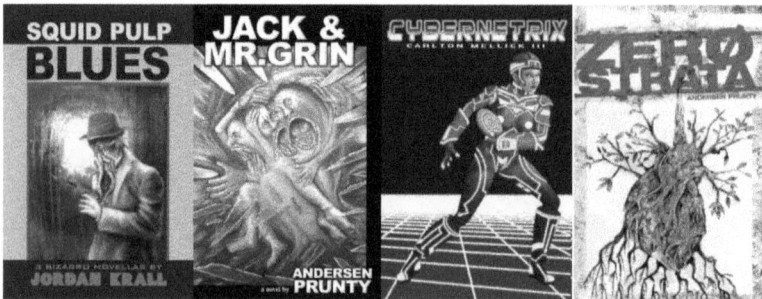

BB-064 "Squid Pulp Blues" Jordan Krall - In these three bizarro-noir novellas, the reader is thrown into a world of murderers, drugs made from squid parts, deformed gun-toting veterans, and a mischievous apocalyptic donkey. **204 pages $12**

BB-065 "Jack and Mr. Grin" Andersen Prunty - "When Mr. Grin calls you can hear a smile in his voice. Not a warm and friendly smile, but the kind that seizes your spine in fear. You don't need to pay your phone bill to hear it. That smile is in every line of Prunty's prose." - Tom Bradley. **208 pages $12**

BB-066 "Cybernetrix" Carlton Mellick III - What would you do if your normal everyday world was slowly mutating into the video game world from Tron? **212 pages $12**

BB-072 "Zerostrata" Andersen Prunty - Hansel Nothing lives in a tree house, suffers from memory loss, has a very eccentric family, and falls in love with a woman who runs naked through the woods every night. **144 pages $11**

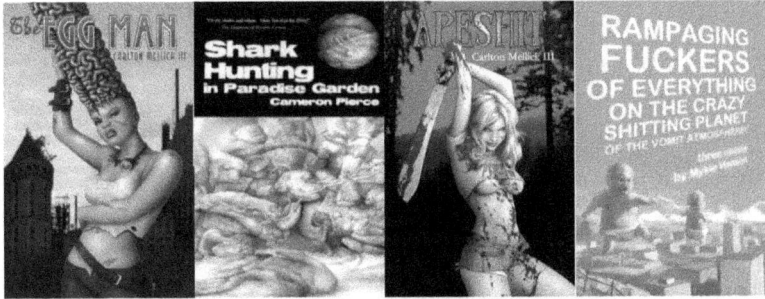

BB-073 "The Egg Man" Carlton Mellick III - It is a world where humans reproduce like insects. Children are the property of corporations, and having an enormous ten-foot brain implanted into your skull is a grotesque sexual fetish. Mellick's industrial urban dystopia is one of his darkest and grittiest to date. **184 pages $11**

BB-074 "Shark Hunting in Paradise Garden" Cameron Pierce - A group of strange humanoid religious fanatics travel back in time to the Garden of Eden to discover it is infested with hundreds of giant flying man-eating sharks. **150 pages $10**

BB-075 "Apeshit" Carlton Mellick III - Friday the 13th meets Visitor Q. Six hipster teens go to a cabin in the woods inhabited by a deformed killer. An incredibly fucked-up parody of B-horror movies with a bizarro slant. **192 pages $12**

BB-076 "Fuckers of Everything on the Crazy Shitting Planet of the Vomit At mosphere" Mykle Hansen - Three bizarro satires. Monster Cocks, Journey to the Center of Agnes Cuddlebottom, and Crazy Shitting Planet. **228 pages $12**

BB-077 "The Kissing Bug" Daniel Scott Buck - In the tradition of Roald Dahl, Tim Burton, and Edward Gorey, comes this bizarro anti-war children's story about a bohemian conenose kissing bug who falls in love with a human woman. **116 pages $10**

BB-078 "MachoPoni" Lotus Rose - It's My Little Pony... *Bizarro* style! A long time ago Poniworld was split in two. On one side of the Jagged Line is the Pastel Kingdom, a magical land of music, parties, and positivity. On the other side of the Jagged Line is Dark Kingdom inhabited by an army of undead ponies. **148 pages $11**

BB-079 "The Faggiest Vampire" Carlton Mellick III - A Roald Dahl-esque children's story about two faggy vampires who partake in a mustache competition to find out which one is truly the faggiest. **104 pages $10**

BB-080 "Sky Tongues" Gina Ranalli - The autobiography of Sky Tongues, the biracial hermaphrodite actress with tongues for fingers. Follow her strange life story as she rises from freak to fame. **204 pages $12**

BB-081 "Washer Mouth" Kevin L. Donihe - A washing machine becomes human and pursues his dream of meeting his favorite soap opera star. **244 pages $11**

BB-082 "Shatnerquake" Jeff Burk - All of the characters ever played by William Shatner are suddenly sucked into our world. Their mission: hunt down and destroy the real William Shatner. **100 pages $10**

BB-083 "The Cannibals of Candyland" Carlton Mellick III - There exists a race of cannibals that are made of candy. They live in an underground world made out of candy. One man has dedicated his life to killing them all. **170 pages $11**

BB-084 "Slub Glub in the Weird World of the Weeping Willows" Andrew Goldfarb - The charming tale of a blue glob named Slub Glub who helps the weeping willows whose tears are flooding the earth. There are also hyenas, ghosts, and a voodoo priest **100 pages $10**

BB-085 "Super Fetus" Adam Pepper - Try to abort this fetus and he'll kick your ass! **104 pages $10**

BB-086 "Fistful of Feet" Jordan Krall - A bizarro tribute to spaghetti westerns, featuring Cthulhu-worshipping Indians, a woman with four feet, a crazed gunman who is obsessed with sucking on candy, Syphilis-ridden mutants, sexually transmitted tattoos, and a house devoted to the freakiest fetishes. **228 pages $12**

BB-087 "Ass Goblins of Auschwitz" Cameron Pierce - It's Monty Python meets Nazi exploitation in a surreal nightmare as can only be imagined by Bizarro author Cameron Pierce. **104 pages $10**

BB-088 "Silent Weapons for Quiet Wars" Cody Goodfellow - "This is high-end psychological surrealist horror meets bottom-feeding low-life crime in a techno-thrilling science fiction world full of Lovecraft and magic..." -John Skipp **212 pages $12**

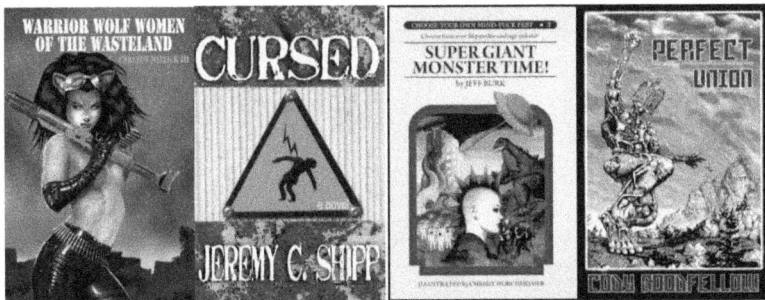

BB-089 "Warrior Wolf Women of the Wasteland" Carlton Mellick III
Road Warrior Werewolves versus McDonaldland Mutants...post-apocalyptic fiction has never been quite like this. **316 pages $13**

BB-090 "Cursed" Jeremy C Shipp - The story of a group of characters who believe they are cursed and attempt to figure out who cursed them and why. A tale of stylish absurdism and suspenseful horror. **218 pages $15**

BB-091 "Super Giant Monster Time" Jeff Burk - A tribute to choose your own adventures and Godzilla movies. Will you escape the giant monsters that are rampaging the fuck out of your city and shit? Or will you join the mob of alien-controlled punk rockers causing chaos in the streets? What happens next depends on you. **188 pages $12**

BB-092 "Perfect Union" Cody Goodfellow - "Cronenberg's THE FLY on a grand scale: human/insect gene-spliced body horror, where the human hive politics are as shocking as the gore." -John Skipp. **272 pages $13**

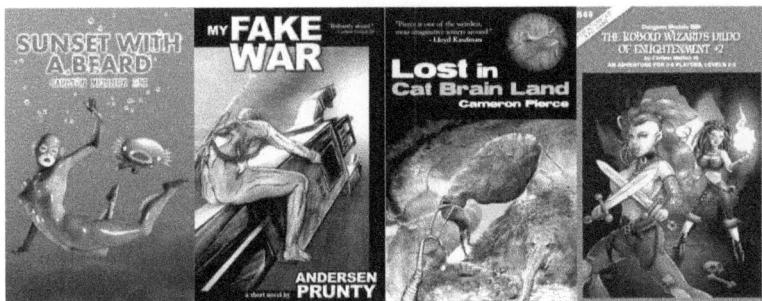

BB-093 "Sunset with a Beard" Carlton Mellick III - 14 stories of surreal science fiction. **200 pages $12**

BB-094 "My Fake War" Andersen Prunty - The absurd tale of an unlikely soldier forced to fight a war that, quite possibly, does not exist. It's Rambo meets Waiting for Godot in this subversive satire of American values and the scope of the human imagination. **128 pages $11**

BB-095 "Lost in Cat Brain Land" Cameron Pierce - Sad stories from a surreal world. A fascist mustache, the ghost of Franz Kafka, a desert inside a dead cat. Primordial entities mourn the death of their child. The desperate serve tea to mysterious creatures. A hopeless romantic falls in love with a pterodactyl. And much more. **152 pages $11**

BB-096 "The Kobold Wizard's Dildo of Enlightenment +2" Carlton Mellick III - A Dungeons and Dragons parody about a group of people who learn they are only made up characters in an AD&D campaign and must find a way to resist their nerdy teenaged players and retarded dungeon master in order to survive. 232 **pages $12**

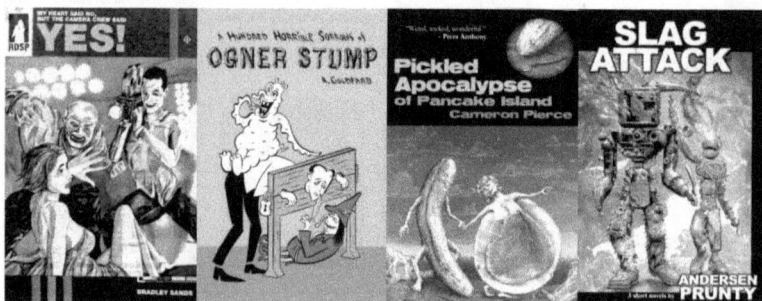

BB-097 "My Heart Said No, but the Camera Crew Said Yes!" Bradley Sands - A collection of short stories that are crammed with the delightfully odd and the scurrilously silly. **140 pages $13**

BB-098 "A Hundred Horrible Sorrows of Ogner Stump" Andrew Goldfarb - Goldfarb's acclaimed comic series. A magical and weird journey into the horrors of everyday life. **164 pages $11**

BB-099 "Pickled Apocalypse of Pancake Island" Cameron Pierce
A demented fairy tale about a pickle, a pancake, and the apocalypse. **102 pages $8**

BB-100 "Slag Attack" Andersen Prunty - Slag Attack features four visceral, noir stories about the living, crawling apocalypse. A slag is what survivors are calling the slug-like maggots raining from the sky, burrowing inside people, and hollowing out their flesh and their sanity. **148 pages $11**

BB-101 "Slaughterhouse High" Robert Devereaux - A place where schools are built with secret passageways, rebellious teens get zippers installed in their mouths and genitals, and once a year, on that special night, one couple is slaughtered and the bits of their bodies are kept as souvenirs. **304 pages $13**

BB-102 "The Emerald Burrito of Oz" John Skipp & Marc Levinthal
OZ IS REAL! Magic is real! The gate is really in Kansas! And America is finally allowing Earth tourists to visit this weird-ass, mysterious land. But when Gene of Los Angeles heads off for summer vacation in the Emerald City, little does he know that a war is brewing...a war that could destroy both worlds. **280 pages $13**

BB-103 "The Vegan Revolution... with Zombies" David Agranoff
When there's no more meat in hell, the vegans will walk the earth. **160 pages $11**

BB-104 "The Flappy Parts" Kevin L Donihe - Poems about bunnies, LSD, and police abuse. You know, things that matter. 132 **pages $11**

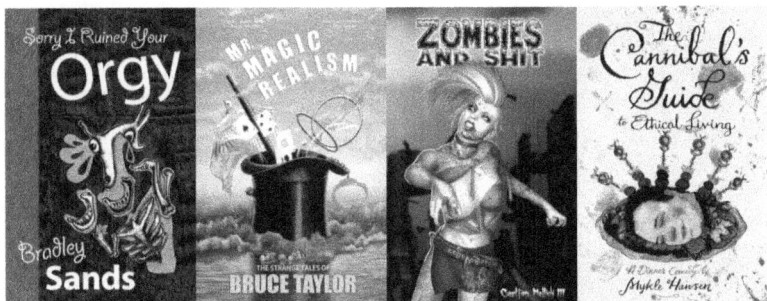

BB-105 "Sorry I Ruined Your Orgy" Bradley Sands - Bizarro humorist Bradley Sands returns with one of the strangest, most hilarious collections of the year. **130 pages $11**

BB-106 "Mr. Magic Realism" Bruce Taylor - Like Golden Age science fiction comics written by Freud, *Mr. Magic Realism* is a strange, insightful adventure that spans the furthest reaches of the galaxy, exploring the hidden caverns in the hearts and minds of men, women, aliens, and biomechanical cats. **152 pages $11**

BB-107 "Zombies and Shit" Carlton Mellick III - "Battle Royale" meets "Return of the Living Dead." Mellick's bizarro tribute to the zombie genre. **308 pages $13**

BB-108 "The Cannibal's Guide to Ethical Living" Mykle Hansen - Over a five star French meal of fine wine, organic vegetables and human flesh, a lunatic delivers a witty, chilling, disturbingly sane argument in favor of eating the rich.. **184 pages $11**

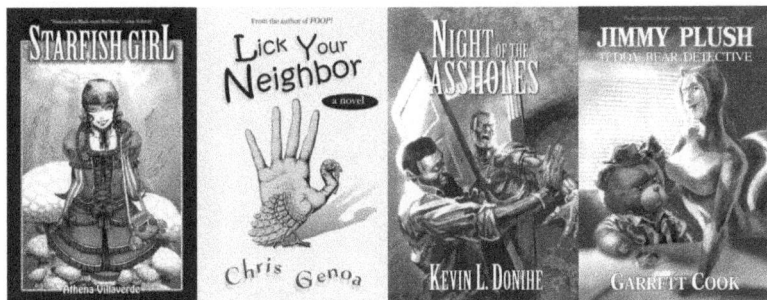

BB-109 "Starfish Girl" Athena Villaverde - In a post-apocalyptic underwater dome society, a girl with a starfish growing from her head and an assassin with sea anenome hair are on the run from a gang of mutant fish men. **160 pages $11**

BB-110 "Lick Your Neighbor" Chris Genoa - Mutant ninjas, a talking whale, kung fu masters, maniacal pilgrims, and an alcoholic clown populate Chris Genoa's surreal, darkly comical and unnerving reimagining of the first Thanksgiving. **303 pages $13**

BB-111 "Night of the Assholes" Kevin L. Donihe - A plague of assholes is infecting the countryside. Normal everyday people are transforming into jerks, snobs, dicks, and douchebags. And they all have only one purpose: to make your life a living hell.. **192 pages $11**

BB-112 "Jimmy Plush, Teddy Bear Detective" Garrett Cook - Hard-boiled cases of a private detective trapped within a teddy bear body. **180 pages $11**

www.ingramcontent.com/pod-product-compliance
Lightning Source LLC
LaVergne TN
LVHW011335080426
835513LV00006B/362